Canon EOS R User Guide

Master Camera Settings, Photo & Video Modes, and Autofocus with Step-by-Step Lessons for Beginners, Seniors & Creators — Includes Real-Life Shooting Tips

Randy Osborn

Disclaimer:

This book is an independent publication and is not affiliated with, authorized, sponsored, or endorsed by Canon Inc. or any of its subsidiaries.

All product names, logos, brands, and trademarks mentioned in this guide are the property of their respective owners. References to "Canon," "Canon EOS R," and any related terms are used strictly for identification and descriptive purposes only, to refer to the camera model that this guide is designed to help users understand and operate.

While every effort has been made to ensure the accuracy and clarity of the information presented, the author and publisher assume no responsibility for errors, omissions, or any outcomes resulting from the application of the techniques or tips described in this book. Camera models, features, software, and firmware updates may change over time. Always consult the official Canon documentation or website for the most current product specifications and instructions.

This guide is intended for educational and informational purposes only.

Table of Contents

Preface

You've got a canon eos r and you want results now. This guide is a friendly, field-ready eos r manual written for real shoots—clear enough for eos r for beginners, practical enough to keep growing. Inside you'll master canon eos r settings, canon eos r autofocus (including face eye detection, one shot servo af, zone af single point), the exposure triangle, aperture shutter iso, and exposure compensation. You'll get low light settings, smarter night photography and long exposure, work with canon log c log, dial 4k video settings and 1080p video settings, pick the right frame rate 24fps 30fps 60fps, build a youtube vlogging setup, and use the video autofocus hunting fix. You'll choose rf lenses beginner, nail portrait settings, landscape settings, travel street photography, wildlife photography, sports action settings, and product photography. You'll set white balance kelvin, tune picture style profile, understand raw vs jpeg, do lightroom snapseed editing, and use sRGB export social media. Plus: overheating fix canon, battery drain fix, wifi pairing canon camera connect, custom modes c1 c2 c3, and troubleshooting blurry photos.

It serves searchers exactly looking for: canon eos r user guide for beginners, canon eos r settings explained step by step, how to use canon eos r autofocus, canon eos r video setup for youtube, best low light settings canon eos r, canon eos r night photography guide, canon eos r long exposure tutorial, canon eos r portrait settings natural skin, eos r landscape sharp focus settings, eos r travel street photography tips, eos r wildlife birds in flight focus, eos r sports action shutter speed, canon eos r product photography lighting, fix blurry photos canon eos r, canon eos r color white balance kelvin, raw editing workflow canon eos r, export settings instagram sRGB, canon eos r overheating solution, canon eos r battery drain solution, canon eos r wifi bluetooth pairing, custom modes c1 c2 c3 canon eos r, eos r seniors simplified camera guide, eos r cheat sheets quick start, eos r menu walkthrough beginners, eos r servo af face tracking, eos r one shot single point portraits, canon rf lens recommendations beginners, canon eos r user guide.

You'll also find: eos r beginners step by step, canon eos r settings quick start, autofocus face eye detection eos r, eos r video 4k 1080p frame rate, low light night long exposure eos r, portraits landscapes travel street tips, canon eos r manual seniors simplified, eos r menu setup custom modes c1 c2 c3, raw vs jpeg color white balance, exposure triangle iso shutter aperture, troubleshooting blurry photos battery wifi, youtube vlogging canon eos r video, wildlife sports product photography guide, canon eos r field guide cheatsheets, eos r autofocus servo one shot zone, canon rf lenses beginner recommendations, export sRGB editing lightroom snapseed, overheating battery drain quick fixes, canon eos r low light indoor settings, travel street photography compact tips.

If you want a guide that feels like a mentor in your camera bag—fast wins, better photos, cleaner video—this is it.

Introduction

You took the leap. You're holding a Canon EOS R—a camera that can make beautiful things—but between the menus, modes, and tiny icons, it's easy to feel like you've adopted a spaceship. This book is your co-pilot. It will not drown you in jargon or demand years of practice before you see results. It will show you exactly what to do in the moment you're about to press the shutter—and why—so your photos and videos start looking the way you imagined when you bought the camera.

Think of this as a field guide written in plain English, with real-world recipes, visual cheat sheets, and problem-solvers. If you've ever said "I just shoot in Auto because everything else is confusing," this is the book that gets you out of Auto—gently, quickly, and for good.

What makes this guide different

- **Field-first, not theory-first.** Every chapter starts with the problem real users face (soft focus, weird color, too much noise) and walks straight to a fix you can try today.

- **Clear, repeatable setups.** You'll get dial moves for portraits, travel, sports, wildlife, products, and video—written so you can follow them with the camera in your hands.

- **Visual help.** Each chapter includes clean, brand-free pictorial explanations you can print or save to your phone for quick reference in the field.

- **Muscle memory over menu diving.** We'll build custom modes and shortcuts so the settings you need live under your fingers, not six menus deep.

- **Beginner-friendly, creator-ready.** Whether you're photographing your kids or shooting YouTube videos, the same principles carry you further than you think.

Who this book is for

- New EOS R owners who want results now without wading through a technical manual.

- Returning photographers who want a modern, mirrorless workflow.

- Content creators who need reliable photo and video settings for real projects.

- Anyone who learns best by doing—with quick wins, practical drills, and checklists.

If you've never left Auto, you're in the right place. If you've dabbled with Av, Tv, or Manual but feel inconsistent, you're also in the right place.

What you'll be able to do by the end

- Set up your EOS R confidently, customize buttons for your style, and find any important setting in two taps.

- Expose correctly on purpose (not by luck), using a simple approach to ISO, shutter speed, and aperture.

- Nail focus—still subjects, moving kids, face/eye detection that behaves, and what to do when it doesn't.

- Shoot video that looks polished (and sounds clean) without a studio or gimbal.

- Handle low light—indoors, night streets, and stars—without turning everything into a noisy blur.

- Store, back up, and edit quickly so your photos don't get trapped on a card or vanish in a folder.

- Keep improving with small, repeatable exercises and creative techniques like long exposures, HDR, and focus stacking.

How the book is organized (and how to use it)

You'll notice a rhythm: Problem → Plain-English Explanation → Do-This-Now Setup → Pictorial Quick Guide → Troubleshooting.

Read straight through if you like, but you'll get the fastest results by using it like this:

1. **Start with Chapters 1–2** to set up the camera and avoid the "I'll just stay in Auto" trap.

2. **Jump to Chapters 3–5** for exposure, autofocus, and video—the core skills that unlock everything else.

3. **Use Chapters 6–9** when you're shooting in specific conditions and scenarios (night, color, family portraits, travel, action, wildlife, product).

4. **Lean on Chapter 10** whenever something goes sideways—power, Wi-Fi, heat, battery, blur.

5. **Chapters 11–12** show you how to finish strong (storage, backup, editing) and how to keep growing (custom modes, long exposure, stacks, HDR, advanced video).

6. **Bonus Cheat Sheets** are one-page, print-friendly recipes and a shortcut chart for fast menu navigation.

Keep the pictorial guides on your phone. Print the cheat sheets and slip them into your bag. When you're out shooting, they're meant to be the "what do I do right now?" answer.

A 15-minute first win

Before you dive into the chapters, try this short routine with your EOS R and the lens you use most:

1. Set Av, aperture f/2.8 (or your widest), Auto ISO, and Minimum Shutter 1/250 **s** in ISO settings.

2. Turn on Face/Eye Detection; leave AF in One-Shot for still people or **Servo** for moving kids/pets.

3. Point someone toward window light. Stand at a comfortable distance.

4. Focus on the near eye, take three frames, and step closer for a tighter portrait.

5. Review at 100%: eyes sharp, skin natural. If not, you'll know exactly which chapter to open next.

That tiny success is the feeling we'll repeat—deliberate choices, predictable results.

What you'll need (and what you don't)

You do not need a bag full of lenses to make wonderful images. Start with whatever you have. A fast prime (like a 50mm f/1.8) or a versatile zoom (24–105mm) is a great partner, but the power comes from settings and light, not price tags. A basic tripod, a cheap wired remote, and a white card or reflector will stretch what you can do. You'll learn where accessories genuinely help—and where they don't.

A note on models, firmware, and names

This guide is written for the Canon EOS R. Menu names can shift slightly with firmware updates, and many techniques apply to other RF bodies. When names differ, use the intent (what we're trying to change) and you'll find the right switch. Throughout the book you'll also see simple, brand-free diagrams so you can recognize the control, even if Canon moves it a tab over in an update.

The promise

You'll never be stuck wondering what to do when the moment is happening in front of you. By the end, you'll have three things most beginners never get:

- **Clarity** about what each setting actually does in your hands.

- **Speed** from custom modes and shortcuts that fit the way you shoot.

- **Confidence** that you can walk into harsh sun, dim rooms, fast action, quiet portraits—or hit record for video—and come away with keepers.

Let's get you there—one simple win at a time.

Chapter 1

Getting Started Without the Overwhelm

You didn't buy the EOS R to become a menu diver. You bought it to make photographs and videos that feel alive. This chapter is your runway: a plain-English tour of the buttons and screens you'll actually touch, a fast menu map to the settings that matter, a first-time setup that prevents 80% of beginner mistakes, and a simple way to leave full Auto behind without anxiety.

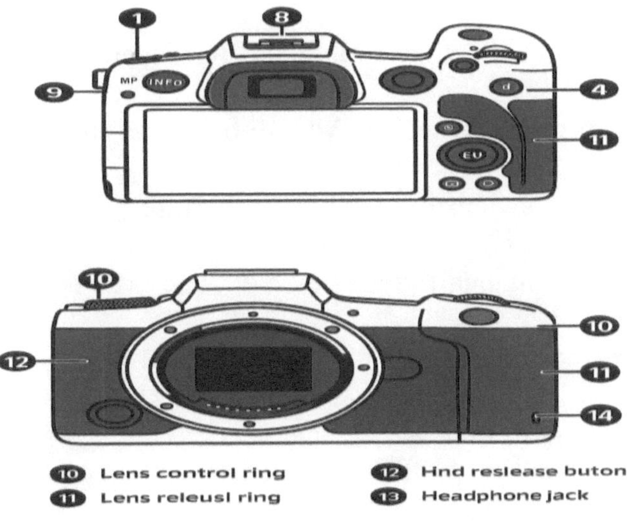

The EOS R in Your Hands (Buttons, Dials, Ports, and Screens—Explained Like a Human)

Forget memorizing names. What matters is *what your fingers do* and *why*.

Right index finger zone (speed):

Shutter button and the main top dial live here. Half-press the shutter to focus, full press to capture. Roll the top dial to change an exposure value (aperture or shutter speed, depending on mode). This is your "don't-think, just shoot" area.

Top deck (awareness):

The small top LCD shows mode, shutter, aperture, ISO, battery—your cockpit at a glance. The MODE button sits nearby; press it and roll a dial to switch between Av (aperture priority), Tv (shutter priority), M (manual), Fv (flexible), and Movie. It's harder to change by accident than a big old-fashioned wheel, which is good once you're used to it.

Rear thumb zone (control):

AF-ON gives you back-button focus—a professional habit that separates focusing from taking the shot. The Q (Quick) button opens a fast, customizable panel so you don't get lost in the full menu. INFO cycles what you see on the screen and in the viewfinder. Playback, Delete, and Menu are here too. You'll use your thumb more than your index finger on this camera.

Touchscreen and EVF (vision):

The fully articulating touchscreen lets you tap to focus, drag focus points, and change settings with the Q screen. The electronic viewfinder (EVF) shows a live preview of exposure and color— what you see is almost what you'll get. There's a tiny diopter wheel by the EVF; if the overlays look fuzzy, adjust that first before blaming the lens.

M-Fn (Multi-Function) button and M-Fn Bar (options):

The small M-Fn button near the shutter can cycle through things like ISO, white balance, and drive mode—set it to your most-used trio.

The touch-sensitive M-Fn bar near the viewfinder is divisive. If you love it, assign a low-risk control like ISO or white balance and require a press-and-hold to activate. If you keep triggering it by accident, disable it. There's no prize for using everything.

Lens and front controls (the optics):

RF lenses have a customizable control ring. Many shooters set it to exposure compensation or ISO for quick, tactile adjustments. The lens release button sits to the side of the mount; press and twist to swap lenses. Treat the mount area like a clean room—cap it if you're not changing lenses quickly.

Ports (connect and monitor):

You'll find a microphone input, headphone jack for monitoring audio, HDMI for an external monitor/recorder, and a USB port for data and tethering. If cables tug, wrap them once around your strap to take strain off the port.

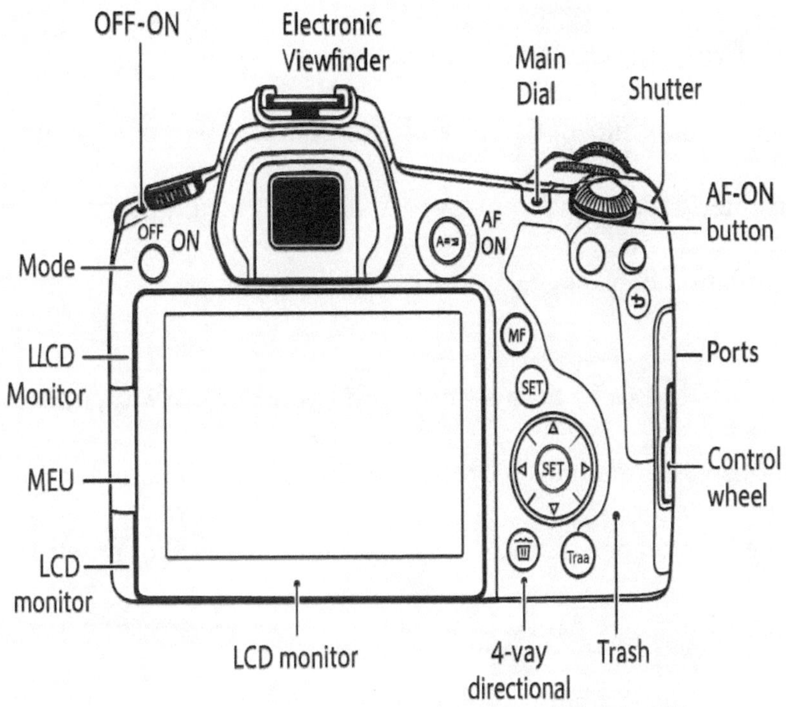

The Menu Tour You'll Actually Remember (Where Essentials Live)

Canon organizes menus into colored tabs. You don't need to memorize everything—just know where to find the "money" settings. Think of these as your homes in each neighborhood.

Red (Shooting) tabs — image quality and exposure behavior:

Set RAW/JPEG, picture style, exposure simulation, drive mode, silent shooting options, and bracketing. If your photos look brighter/darker in the EVF than the result, check exposure simulation here.

Purple/Red (AF) tabs — how the camera finds sharpness:

Choose AF method (Face + Tracking, Zone, 1-Point), turn Eye Detection on or off, and set AF operation (One-Shot for still scenes, Servo for movement). If your camera keeps grabbing the wrong subject, this is where you fix it.

Blue (Playback) tabs — how you review:

Enable highlight alerts ("blinkies") so blown areas flash in review. Turn on a histogram if you like reading exposure curves instead of guessing.

Yellow (Wrench/Setup) tabs — housekeeping:

Date/time, sensor cleaning, card formatting, screen brightness, Wi-

Fi/Bluetooth, power saving, and firmware updates. It's the utility closet—boring but essential.

Orange (Custom Function/Customize) tabs — make it *your* camera:

Assign buttons, dial directions, control ring behavior, back-button focus, shutter/AE lock preferences, touch & drag AF, and custom shooting modes (C1–C3). If something feels awkward, this is where you reshape it.

Green (My Menu) — your personal dashboard:

Pin the items you change often: Format Card, Eye Detection AF, ISO speed settings, Movie Rec quality, Sensor Cleaning. One screen, zero hunting.

First-Time Setup That Prevents Headaches Later (A Ten-Minute Checklist)

Grab a charged battery and a memory card you're willing to format. Work through this once; it will pay you back every time you press the shutter.

1. **Set the date, time, and time zone.** Your edits and backups will line up with your phone and computer later.

2. **Adjust the EVF diopter.** Look at the *text overlays* in the EVF and spin the tiny wheel until the text looks razor sharp. If the overlays are sharp, your eye is calibrated to the finder.

3. **Format the card in-camera.** This creates a clean folder structure the camera expects.

4. **Choose image quality.**

   - If you edit, select RAW or C-RAW for smaller files with excellent latitude.

o   If you don't edit, select JPEG Fine.

   One is not morally superior. Pick what matches your workflow.

5. **Pick a picture style.** Start with Standard for a pleasing baseline. If you plan to grade video or edit heavily, choose a flatter profile for capture, not for show-and-go.

6. **Enable exposure simulation.** Seeing a near-final brightness in the EVF builds intuition and reduces "why is it dark?" surprises.

7. **Autofocus setup that just works.**

   o   AF Method: Face + Tracking for people and general use.

   o   Eye Detection: On.

   o   AF Operation: One-Shot for still subjects; Servo for motion. You will toggle this often.

8. **Pick your starter exposure mode.**

   o   Av (Aperture Priority) if you care most about background blur and overall look.

- Fv (Flexible Priority) if you want one place to control shutter, aperture, and ISO with the option to leave any of them on Auto.

  M (Manual) is fantastic once you have a feel; you don't need it on Day 1 to be "real."

9. **Set Auto ISO with a reasonable ceiling.** Start with a max of ISO 6400. You'll get more keepers in dim places without worrying every second about noise.

10. **Turn on a safety net for brightness.** Make exposure compensation easy to reach (via the control ring or rear dial) so you can nudge the scene brighter or darker without menu diving.

11. **Customize buttons minimally.**

    - AF-ON: back-button focus.

    - *AE-Lock*: lock exposure when recomposing.

    - M-Fn button: cycle ISO → white balance → drive mode.

    Keep the map simple and consistent.

12. **Decide the fate of the M-Fn bar.** If you graze it by accident, set it to require a press-and-hold or disable it. Zero shame in turning it off.

13. **Set up the Q screen.** Add the things you change often: AF method, Eye AF, ISO, white balance, picture style, drive mode, resolution/frame rate for video.

14. **Create one Custom Mode (C1) for your most common scenario.**

    For example, "Family Portraits": Av, f/2.8, Face/Eye AF on, Auto ISO, +0.3 EV, single shot. Save it. Now you have a safety preset.

15. **Turn on highlight alerts in playback.** If the sky blinks white, dial negative exposure compensation and reshoot.

16. **Do a quick audio/video sanity check.** Plug in a mic if you have one, set 1080p at 24/30 fps to start, enable continuous AF, and record a ten-second clip. If you can hear clearly and the focus doesn't hunt, you're good.

Ten minutes, and your camera is set up like a patient, competent assistant.

Quick Wins in the Real World (Two Tiny Missions)

You learn by doing. These are designed to work *today* with the kit you already own.

Mission 1: A flattering portrait near a window

Set Av. Choose f/2.8–f/4 if your lens allows. Face + Eye AF on. Auto ISO. Turn your subject slightly toward the window and step closer than feels comfortable. Focus on the eye, add +0.3 exposure compensation if the skin looks dull, and take three frames. You'll see crisp eyes, gentle background blur, and healthy color without touching a flash.

Mission 2: A clean street or travel scene

Set Av at f/5.6–f/8 for deeper focus. Use Zone AF or a movable point to anchor your subject. Auto ISO. Compose with a foreground element (railing, signage) to add depth. Wait for a person to step into the frame to offer scale and story. Review and adjust exposure compensation by a third of a stop if needed.

These two exercises build instincts that translate everywhere.

Leaving Full Auto Behind (Without Panic)

Auto is comforting until it isn't. It chooses a safe, generic look and sometimes drags your shutter speed too low, pumps the ISO too high, or misreads a backlit scene. You don't need to quit cold turkey; you just need one *friendly* mode and two mental models.

Friendly mode: Av (Aperture Priority) or Fv (Flexible Priority).

- In **Av**, you pick the look with aperture, the camera chooses shutter speed, and Auto ISO fills in the rest. If faces are dark, tap +0.3 to +0.7 exposure compensation. If the sky blows out, tap −0.3 to −1.0.

- In **Fv**, you can set any one (or two) variables and leave the others on Auto in one unified place. It's manual training wheels, minus the wobbles.

Two mental models you'll actually use:

1. **Depth vs. motion.**

   Ask, "Do I care more about background blur or freezing movement?"

   If blur: open the aperture (small f-number). If motion: raise shutter speed. Let ISO float.

2. **Nudge, don't wrestle.**

   Exposure compensation is your "whisper to the camera"—a small nudge toward brighter or darker. It's faster and less stressful than trying to fix everything at once.

AF mode swapping without fear:

- Still subject? One-Shot AF + a single point or Face/Eye detect.

- Moving subject? Servo AF + Face/Eye or a small zone. If the camera struggles in tricky light, switch briefly to manual focus, use focus peaking, nail it, and switch back. Pro shooters do this all the time.

Common Early Problems and the One-Move Fix

- **"My photos are soft."** Check the EVF diopter first. Then go One-Shot + single point on a high-contrast edge (an eye or collar), and keep shutter speed at least 1/125s for people.

- **"Colors look weird indoors."** Change white balance from Auto to Tungsten/Incandescent under warm bulbs, or step nearer to window light.

- **"Everything looks noisy."** Noise is often under-exposure. Add +0.3 to +0.7 exposure compensation, then lower ISO later if needed.

- **"It's blurry at night."** Open the aperture, raise ISO to 3200–6400, and lean against a wall. If subjects move, use Servo AF and keep shutter 1/250s or faster.

- **"Menus overwhelm me."** Live on the Q screen and My Menu. You only need five or six items daily. The rest can wait.

Small Habits, Big Confidence

- Format cards in-camera after backing up.

- Keep one custom mode for your go-to scenario and update it as you learn.

- Clean the front element with a blower and a microfiber cloth before a big day.

- Review at 100% and check for sharp eyes, not just overall brightness.

- Shoot for five minutes a few evenings each week—your living room is a perfectly good classroom.

UNDERSTANDING THE CANON EOS R LAYOUT
Front, Top, and Rear Views

FRONT VIEW

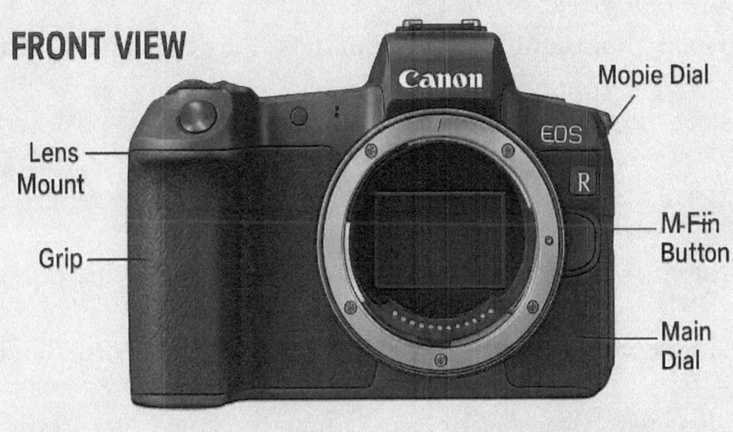

TOP VIEW

REAR VIEW

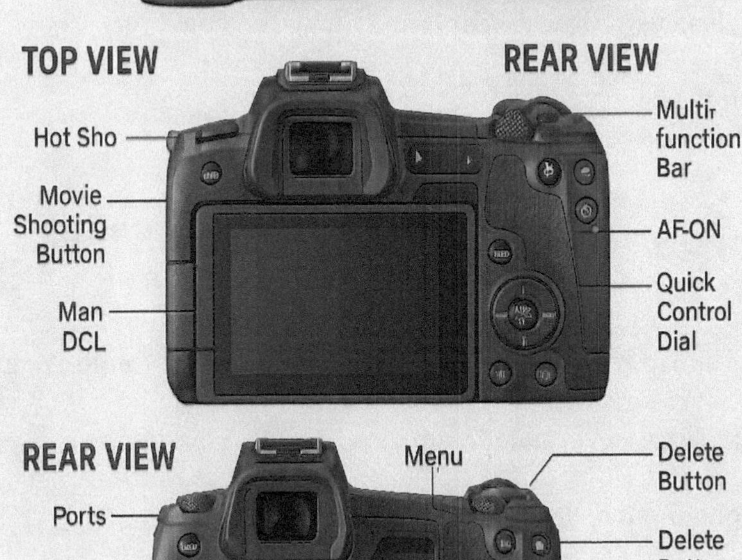

47

Chapter 2

Setting Up for Success

Great photos don't come from luck; they come from a camera that's been set up to help you. This chapter gives you a smart, forgiving startup configuration you can apply in minutes. You'll get defaults for stills and video, clarity on RAW vs. JPEG and color profiles, a simple control layout that matches how you actually shoot, and a clean workflow for cards and folders so your images never disappear into chaos.

A rock-solid default for stills

Think of this as your everyday "it just works" setup. You can tweak it later, but start here and you'll make sharp, well-exposed photographs in almost any ordinary scene.

Exposure mode

- **Av (Aperture Priority)** or **Fv (Flexible Priority)**.

  Av keeps the look (depth of field) in your hands while the camera handles shutter. Fv is even friendlier: you can set any item you care about and let the rest float.

Aperture

- People, food, details: start around f/2.8–f/4 for soft backgrounds.

- Scenes, travel, groups: f/5.6–f/8 for deeper focus.

ISO

- **Auto ISO** with a maximum of 6400. This keeps shutter speeds comfortably high without wrecking files with extreme noise.

Shutter minimum

- If your lens or subject tends to blur, set a Minimum Shutter Speed of about 1/125s for people, 1/250s for kids/pets, 1/500s+ for sports.

Metering

- **Evaluative** (multi-segment). It's consistent and predictable for mixed lighting.

Autofocus

- **AF Method: Face + Tracking** for general use.
- **Eye Detection: On** for portraits.
- **AF Operation: One-Shot** for still subjects; Servo for motion. You'll swap this often—make it quick to reach.

Drive mode

- **Single shot** for most photos. Switch to High-speed continuous when moments move fast.

White balance

- **Auto** to begin. If indoor bulbs go orange, switch to Tungsten/Incandescent; outdoors shade looks cool, so try Shade or add + Warmth.

Picture style

- If you shoot RAW, the style doesn't lock you in—Standard is fine.
- If you shoot JPEG, try Standard for general use or Neutral if you hate over-punchy color.

Stabilization

- Leave lens IS On for handheld stills. Turn it Off on a tripod.

Exposure simulation

- On so the viewfinder shows a near-final brightness before you click.

Highlight alert (blinkies)

- On for playback. If skies blink, dial a little negative exposure compensation and reshoot.

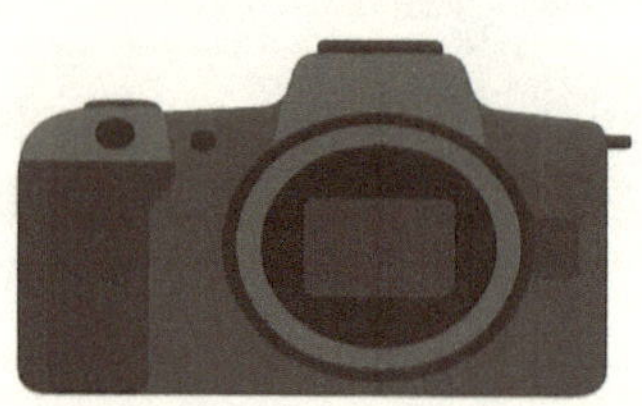

A worry-free default for video

Video punishes hesitation. Set a simple baseline that looks clean and keeps focus nailed.

Resolution & frame rate

- Start with 1080p at 24p for a cinematic feel or 30p for general use.

- 60p is great if you plan to slow footage to half-speed.

- Use 4K when you need extra detail or cropping room; it demands more card speed and storage.

Shutter speed

- Follow the easy rule: shutter ≈ 1 / (2 × frame rate). 24p → 1/50s, 30p → 1/60s, 60p → 1/125s. This keeps motion natural.

Autofocus

- **Movie Servo AF: On**.

- **Face/Eye Detection:** On for people and talking-head clips.

- If AF "breathes," reduce AF speed/sensitivity slightly in Movie AF settings for steadier pulls.

Stabilization

- **Lens IS: On**.

- If available, Movie Digital IS: Standard; turn it Off on a tripod.

Picture style

- If you won't color-grade, use Standard (pleasant straight from camera).

- If you will grade, choose Neutral or a flatter look to save highlights.

Audio

- Plug in a small external mic if you own one; set Sound Recording to Manual and adjust levels so peaks hit around the meter's safe zone without clipping.

- Use Wind Filter/Attenuator when outdoors and the audio overloads.

Practical shooting habit

- Hold each shot for 5 full seconds before moving the camera.

Your editor (even if that's just you) will thank you.

DEFAULT VIDEO SETUP

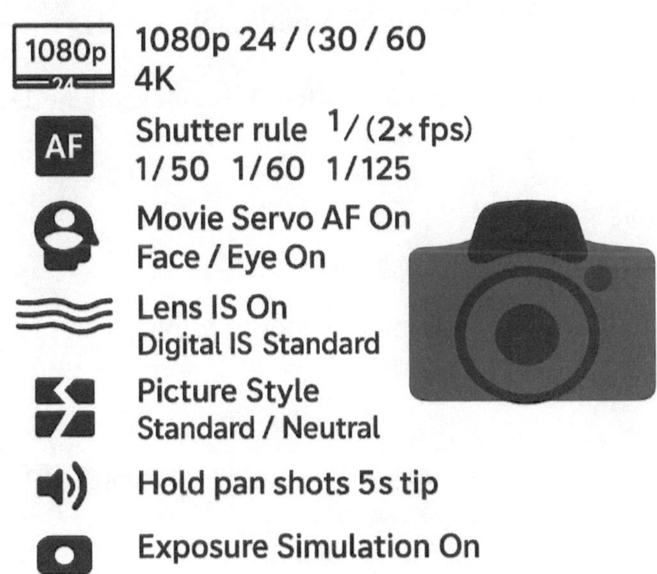

RAW vs. JPEG (and when C-RAW makes sense)

RAW gives you the most freedom later—more room to fix exposure, white balance, and shadows. Files are bigger, and you'll edit before sharing.

JPEG is light, fast, and ready to post. What you see is close to what you get; there's less latitude for dramatic fixes.

C-RAW (Canon's compressed RAW) is a sweet spot on the EOS R. It keeps RAW flexibility with noticeably smaller file sizes. Unless you're doing extreme edits, C-RAW is an excellent default.

Use this simple rule:

- If you love editing or shoot in tricky light, pick RAW or C-RAW.
- If you want speed and simplicity, pick JPEG and keep exposure close to perfect in-camera.

Color space for stills

- sRGB for the web and general use.
- Adobe RGB if your destination is print and you work in color-managed apps. If you're unsure, sRGB is safer.

White balance and skin tones

- In RAW, you can correct later, so works well.

- In JPEG, choose a specific WB when light is consistent (Daylight, Shade, Tungsten) to avoid color swings across a

DEFAULT VIDEO SETUP

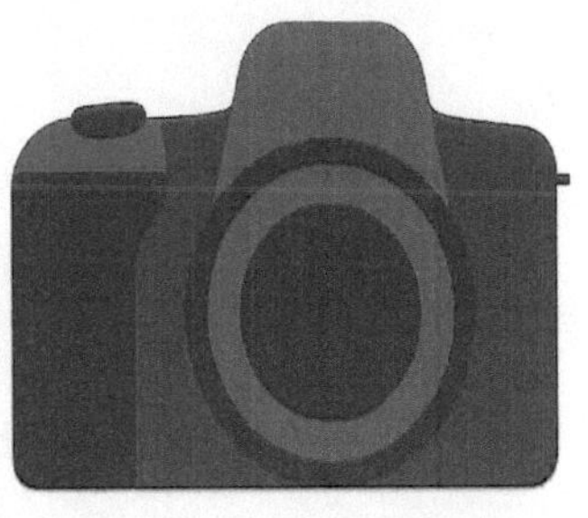

100 1080p 24/10s

4K 4K

✓ 1/(2×) shutter rule 1/(2× fps) 1/15s

✓ Movie Servo AF On

✓ Face/Eye On

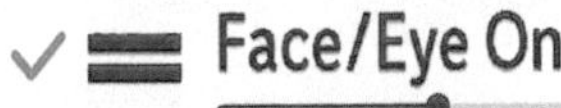

✓ Lens IS On   External mic with manual levels

✓ Digital IS Standard   Wind shots 5s tip

✓ External mic   Hold shots 5s

✓ Exposure Simulation On

Choose a color profile you won't regret

Color profiles (Picture Styles) don't change RAW data, but they do change JPEGs and the preview you judge while shooting.

- **Standard**: natural contrast and color; great default.

- **Portrait**: gentler contrast for skin; nice for faces.

- **Neutral**: lower contrast and saturation; preserves highlights for later editing.

- **Fine Detail**: subtle sharpening for textures.

For video, if you're not grading, Standard is perfectly fine. If you plan to grade, Neutral gives you extra headroom in bright scenes.

Customizing buttons for the way you shoot

The goal is to make important actions muscle memory. Keep it simple; three or four great assignments beat a dozen you forget.

Back-button focus

- Set AF-ON to focus and the shutter button to meter/shoot. This prevents accidental refocus as you press the shutter and is a huge win for sharpness.

AE-Lock

- Map the * button to lock exposure while you recompose. Helpful for backlit portraits and bright windows.

M-Fn button

- Cycle your "daily three": ISO → White Balance → Drive Mode. One press, one twist—done.

Lens Control Ring

- Assign Exposure Compensation or ISO. It's tactile and fast without pulling your eye from the viewfinder.

Touch & drag AF

- Enable it so you can slide the focus point with your thumb on the screen while looking through the EVF. It feels like using a trackpad—very precise once you try it.

M-Fn Bar

- If it causes accidental changes, require a press-and-hold or turn it off. Zero penalty for choosing reliability.

Q screen

- Add tiles you actually change: AF Method, Eye Detection, ISO, WB, Picture Style, Drive, Resolution/FPS. Remove anything you never touch to de-clutter.

Custom Modes (C1–C3)

- Save full setups you need often. For example:

  C1 — Family Portraits: Av, f/2.8, Face/Eye On, One-Shot, Auto ISO max 6400, +0.3 EV, Single shot.

  C2 — Action/Kids: Tv 1/1000s, Servo AF, Zone AF, Auto

ISO max 12800, High-speed burst.

C3 — Talking-Head Video: 1080p/30p, 1/60s, Movie Servo AF On, Face/Eye On, Picture Style Standard, Audio Manual with levels set, Digital IS Standard.

Once saved, you can twist to a custom mode and start shooting without rebuilding settings from memory.

Card speed, formatting, and a bulletproof folder habit

A clean card and a predictable folder system are the difference between "organized photographer" and "where did my files go?"

Card choice

- Use a reputable U3 / V30 SD card at minimum for video and burst stills. Larger capacities (64–128 GB) reduce mid-shoot swaps.

Always format in-camera

- After backing up, format the card in the EOS R, not your computer. The camera builds the exact folder structure it expects and prevents weird file errors.

Don't delete files in-camera

- Deleting one-by-one during a shoot risks corrupting the directory if the battery dies. Leave culling for your computer or phone app later.

"Create New Folder" at logical breaks

- Starting a new day, location, or client? Use the camera's Create New Folder. It makes importing and sorting cleaner.

File numbering

- Set Continuous numbering so file names don't reset and collide on your computer. If you truly need a fresh sequence, use Manual Reset right before a new project.

Import and rename on the computer

- Use a simple, sortable pattern such as

  `YYYY-MM-DD_Project_####.CR3`

  or

  `YYYYMMDD_HHMMSS_Custom.CR3`

  This keeps images in chronological order and prevents duplicate file names across cameras.

Three-layer backup habit (3-2-1 rule)

- **3 copies** of your photos, 2 different media, 1 off-site (cloud or a drive in another location). It sounds formal, but it's just: computer → external drive → cloud. Set it once and forget it.

Card retirement

- Cards wear out. If a card ever throws errors, retire it immediately. Label new cards with a tiny sticker and keep a simple rotation so you know which ones are oldest.

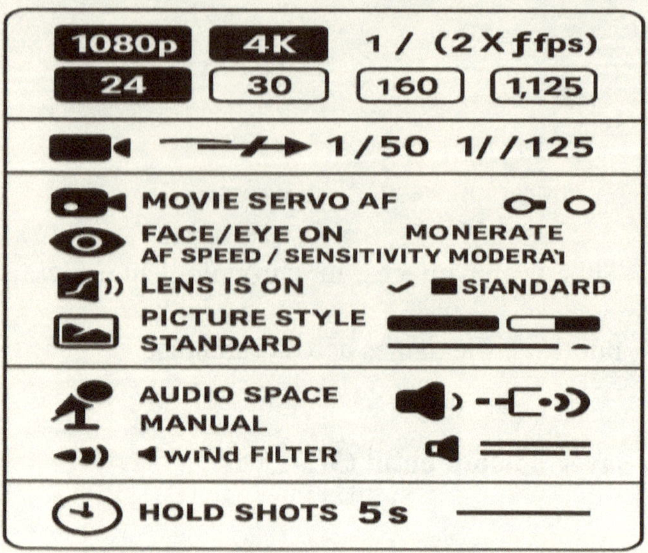

A five-minute stills setup you can trust

1. Av or Fv selected.

2. Auto ISO with max 6400 and a sensible Minimum Shutter.

3. Evaluative metering; exposure simulation On.

4. Face + Tracking with Eye Detection On; One-Shot for still subjects.

5. Picture Style Standard (RAW/C-RAW shooters don't stress).

6. Highlight alert On; Q screen customized; AF-ON for focus.

7. Save your "everyday" to C1.

A five-minute video setup you can repeat

1. 1080p at 24/30p (60p if you'll slow-mo).

2. Shutter near 1/50, 1/60, or 1/125 respectively.

3. Movie Servo AF On; Face/Eye On; AF speed/sensitivity modest.

4. Picture Style Standard (or Neutral if grading).

5. Lens IS On, Digital IS Standard unless on tripod.

6. External mic if available; set audio manually.

7. Save to C3.

What this chapter fixes—permanently

- You won't fight blur because your shutter and AF are aligned with your subject.

- You won't fear dim rooms because Auto ISO is capped sensibly and exposure comp is at your fingertips.

- Your video won't look like a test clip because focus, shutter, and audio are under control.

- You won't lose files to chaos because cards are formatted properly and folders are predictable.

- Your hands will do the same moves every time, which means you can think about light and story instead of menus.

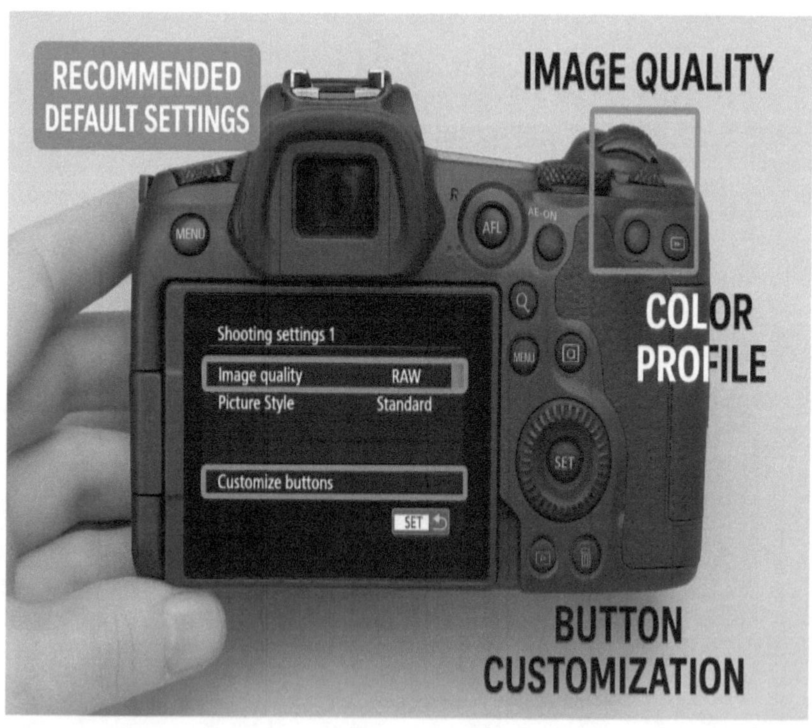

Chapter 3

Mastering Exposure Made Simple

If Chapter 2 set up your camera to help you, this one trains your eyes. Exposure isn't magic; it's three simple levers—aperture, shutter speed, ISO—that decide how bright the picture is and *how* it looks. Once you understand what each lever does to your photo, you stop guessing and start making choices.

The Exposure Triangle in Plain English

Aperture (the opening in the lens)

- **What it does to light:** A wider opening lets in more light; a smaller opening lets in less.

- **What it does to look:** Controls background blur (depth of field).

- o **Wide aperture** like f/1.8–f/2.8 = bright + creamy background blur.

- o **Narrow aperture** like f/8–f/16 = darker + more of the scene in focus.

- **What to remember:** Think "aperture = blur."

Shutter Speed (how long light hits the sensor)

- **What it does to light:** Longer time = brighter; shorter time = darker.

- **What it does to look:** Controls motion.

  - o **Fast** shutter like 1/1000s freezes action.

  - o **Slow** shutter like 1/15s shows motion blur (or handshake).

- **What to remember:** Think "shutter = motion."

ISO (sensor sensitivity)

- **What it does to light:** Higher ISO makes the sensor more sensitive; the image brightens.

- **What it does to look:** Adds **noise** (grain).

  - ○ **Low** ISO like 100–200 = clean.

  - ○ **High** ISO like 3200–12800 = brighter in dark places, but grainier.

- **What to remember:** Think "ISO = brightness backup." Use it to save the shot when light is low or your shutter must be fast.

Put simply: aperture shapes blur, shutter shapes motion, and ISO fills in the brightness when the other two are where you want them.

How They Work Together (feel it, don't memorize it)

Imagine filling a bucket:

- **Aperture** is how wide the tap is.

- **Shutter speed** is how long it's open.

- **ISO** is the water pressure.

If the scene is too dark, you can open the tap wider (lower f-number), leave it open longer (slower shutter), or increase the pressure (raise ISO). The trick is choosing the one that also gives you the *look* you want.

Real-World Examples You Can Copy

Use these as starting points, then nudge based on the light in front of you. Keep Auto ISO on with a sensible maximum (e.g., 6400) so you're not stuck when light drops.

1) Portraits with creamy background

- **Mode:** Av (Aperture Priority)
- **Aperture:** f/2.8–f/4 (wider if your lens allows)
- **Shutter:** Camera chooses; make sure it stays above ~1/125s for adults, 1/250s for kids
- **ISO:** Auto
- **AF:** Face/Eye Detection On

- **Why it works:** The wide aperture isolates your subject; Auto ISO keeps exposure sweet without stealing your attention.

- **Common fix:** If faces look dull in backlit scenes, add **+0.3 to +0.7** exposure compensation.

2) Action shots (sports, kids running, pets)

- **Mode:** Tv (Shutter Priority) or Fv (set shutter and let the rest float)

- **Shutter:** 1/1000s (outdoor daylight) or 1/500s if light is limited

- **Aperture:** Camera chooses (often wide open)

- **ISO:** Auto, max 12800 if indoors

- **AF:** Servo + Zone/Tracking

- **Why it works:** The fast shutter freezes motion; Auto ISO rises to keep brightness.

3) Landscapes with detail front to back

- **Mode:** Av

- **Aperture:** f/8 (go to f/11 only if you truly need more depth)

- **Shutter:** Camera chooses—use a tripod if it gets slow

- **ISO:** 100–200 for the cleanest file

- **AF:** Single point on a subject about one-third into the scene

- **Why it works:** Narrower aperture deepens focus across the frame without pushing ISO.

4) Indoors at home (no flash)

- **Mode:** Av

- **Aperture:** f/2–f/4

- **Shutter minimum:** 1/125s to avoid blur

- **ISO:** Auto (the camera may go to 3200–6400—okay)

- **White Balance:** Auto or Tungsten if everything is orange

- **Why it works:** You keep blur under control with aperture while ISO quietly saves the moment.

5) Night streets or creative motion blur

- **Mode:** M or Fv

- **Shutter:** 1/10s to 1s depending on how much blur you want

- **Aperture:** f/4–f/8

- **ISO:** As low as possible (100–800) for cleaner files

- **Stability:** Brace on a wall or use a tripod

- **Why it works:** Slow shutter draws light trails and movement; low ISO keeps noise down.

Exposure Compensation: Your Gentle Steering Wheel

Your camera aims for middle gray—it tries to average a scene to a safe mid-tone. That's fine until you shoot snow, beaches, backlit faces, or dark subjects on dark backgrounds. In those cases, the meter guesses wrong.

Exposure compensation is your fast correction. You're not arguing with the camera—you're *whispering* what you prefer.

- **Make it brighter (+):** Backlit portraits, white walls, beaches, snow. Start with +0.3 to +1.0.

- **Make it darker (–):** Shiny highlights, stage lights, bright skies with important clouds. Start with –0.3 to –1.0.

Watch the EVF preview and the blinkies in playback:

- If important areas flash white, you're blowing highlights—dial a little minus and reshoot.

- If everything looks muddy and dull, tap plus.

The goal isn't a perfect histogram; it's a photo that holds detail where *you* care about it.

Reading Light Without Fear

A quick checklist you can run in two seconds:

1. **Where is the brightest area I care about?** (sky, forehead, white dress)

   Protect it—if it clips to pure white, it's gone. Use a bit of minus compensation or angle slightly.

2. **Do I want blur or detail in the background?**

   Choose aperture first based on that answer.

3. **Is anything moving?**

   If yes, pick a shutter that fits: 1/500s for kids, 1/1000s for fast action, slower if you want intentional blur.

4. **Let ISO do the housekeeping.**

   Auto ISO is your assistant. Cap it high enough that the camera won't choose a dangerously slow shutter in dim rooms.

That's exposure in real life: protect bright stuff, choose blur or motion, then let ISO support you.

Practical Exercises to Lock It In

Exercise A — The Aperture Walk

Pick one small scene (a plant on a table by a window). Photograph it at f/2.8, f/4, f/5.6, f/8 from the same spot.

- **What to notice:** How the background changes from creamy to detailed.

- **Tip:** Keep the focus on the same leaf. Review at 100% and feel the difference.

Aperture

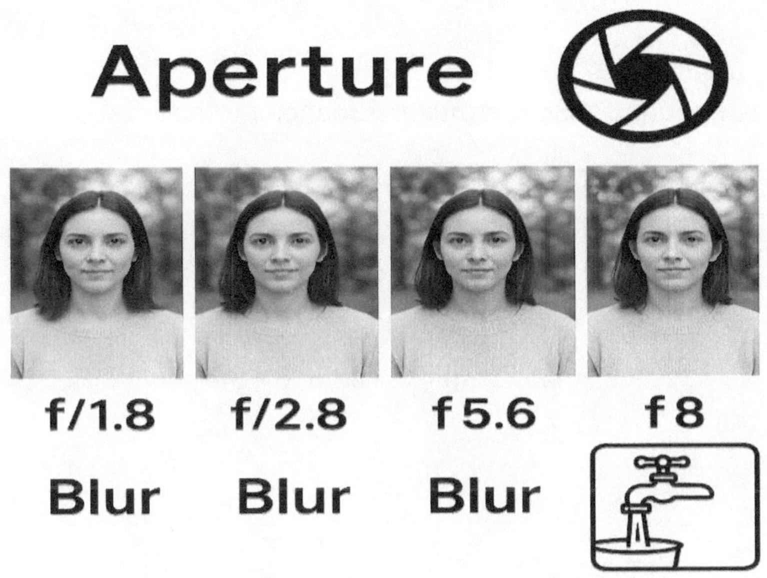

Exercise B — Freeze vs. Flow

Go outside where people or cars pass.

- Shoot **1/1000s** to freeze motion.

- Shoot **1/30s** while panning with the moving subject.

- Shoot **1/10s** to turn the background into streaks.

- **What to notice:** How shutter speed changes the *story* of the scene.

Exercise C — ISO Tolerance Test

In a dim room, keep aperture and shutter constant. Take frames at
ISO 400, 800, 1600, 3200, 6400.

- **What to notice:** How grain appears, and where you
  personally stop caring. Everyone's threshold differs; find
  yours.

Exercise D — Compensation Confidence

Find backlight: a window with your subject in front, or a lamp
behind an object.

- Start at **0.0** EV.

- Make a frame at **+0.3, +0.7, +1.0**.

- Make another at **–0.3, –0.7** for comparison.

- **What to notice:** How skin and detail shift. Pick your
  favorite and remember that number for similar situations.

On a bright day, point at a scene with clouds.

- Dial **–0.7** EV and shoot.

- Then shoot at **0.0** EV.

- **What to notice:** The minus version holds cloud texture; you can brighten shadows later.

Do these once, and exposure stops feeling like math and starts feeling like taste.

Troubleshooting Bright/Dark Photos—Fast Fixes

- **Faces are too dark with a bright background:** Add **+0.7 EV**, move your subject closer to the light source, or turn them slightly toward it.

- **Skies are pure white:** Use **–0.7 EV**, angle the camera a touch down, or try a narrower aperture and lower ISO.

- **Indoor photos are yellow/blue:** Switch White Balance to Tungsten indoors or Daylight by a window; remember you can fix WB later if you shot RAW.

- **Everything is blurry at night:** Raise ISO to 3200–6400, open the aperture, and keep shutter at 1/125s or faster for people. Brace yourself or use a tripod for slower speeds.

A Simple Way to Practice Every Week

Give yourself five minutes, once a week, with one subject:

1. Decide blur vs. detail → choose aperture.

2. Decide freeze vs. flow → choose shutter.

3. Let Auto ISO handle brightness.

4. Use exposure compensation to taste.

5. Make three frames with tiny changes and pick the one you love.

Aperture

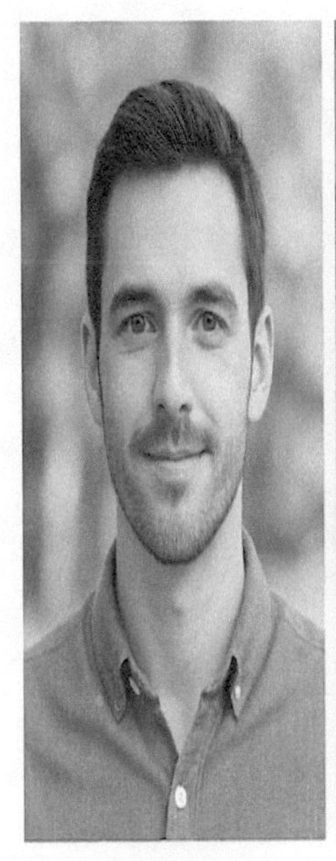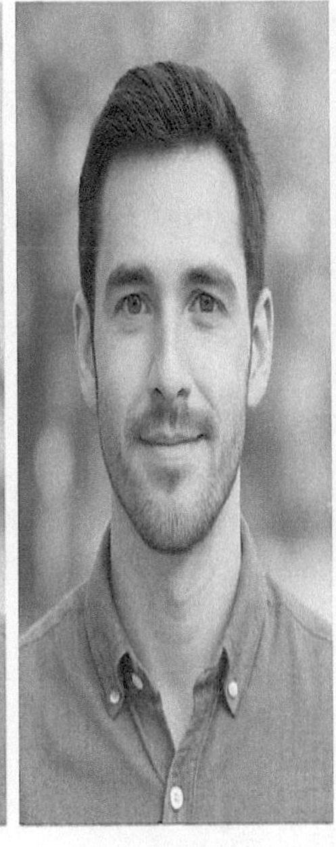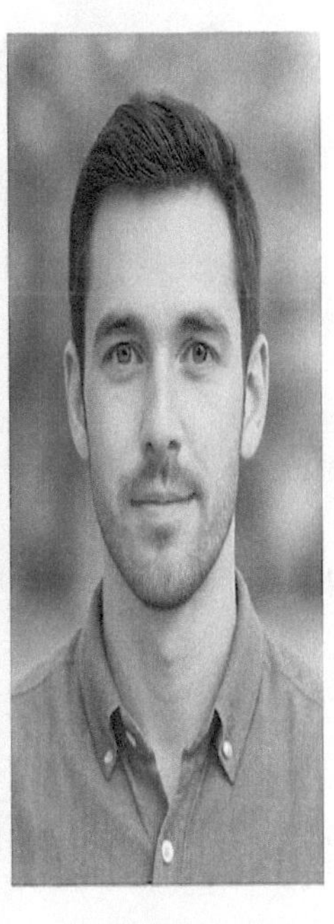

f/1.8   f/2.8   f/5.6

Chapter 4

Autofocus Demystified

Missed focus feels personal—like the camera ignored you. It didn't. It only followed the instructions it was given. In this chapter you'll learn, in plain language, which instructions to give: when to lock focus once, when to keep tracking, when to take control by hand, and how to choose the right focus area so the camera grabs the *thing* you care about—an eye, a runner, a bird against a busy background. By the end, soft images should be the rare exception.

How the EOS R actually focuses (the 10-second version)

Your EOS R uses Dual Pixel autofocus. Each pixel on the sensor helps measure phase (direction) so it knows *which way* and *how far* to move focus. Translation: it's fast and accurate—if you tell it what to prioritize. That's your job.

One-Shot, Servo, Manual — which and why

One-Shot AF

- **What it does:** Locks focus once when you half-press the shutter or press AF-ON.

- **Use it for:** Still subjects—portraits that hold, products on a table, landscapes, architecture.

- **Benefit:** Precise; you can recompose after locking focus.

- **Watch out:** If your subject moves or you move, focus can slip—especially with wide apertures.

Servo AF

- **What it does:** Continuously adjusts focus while you half-press or hold AF-ON.

- **Use it for:** Anything that can move—kids, pets, street, sports, events.

- **Benefit:** Tracks motion so you don't have to refocus every frame.

- **Watch out:** Needs a good target to track. If the subject is tiny or blocked, it may jump to the background.

Manual Focus (MF)

- **What it does:** You turn the ring, the camera doesn't hunt.

- **Use it for:** Macro, shooting through glass/fences, backlit silhouettes, low-contrast subjects, precise video pulls.

- **Benefit:** Absolute control. With focus peaking and magnify, it's easier than you think.

- **Watch out:** Slower until you build the feel. Use peaking/magnify so you're not guessing.

A simple habit: One-Shot for still; Servo for moving; MF when the camera can't see what you see.

AF AREA MODES

Face+Tracking	Zone AF	1-Point AF
Use for portraits, subjects in motion	Use for tracking groups, intermediate areas	Use for stationary subjects
Use for portraits	Use for stationary	

Choosing the right AF area (where the camera is allowed to look)

Think of area modes as the size of the net you cast.

Face + Tracking

- **What it does:** Finds faces/eyes and follows subjects across the frame.

- **Use it for:** People, interviews, vlogging, casual everyday shooting.

- **Avoid when:** Faces are tiny, turned away, or there are many faces you don't want. Switch to a smaller area for control.

Zone AF

- **What it does:** A medium-sized box. The camera prioritizes subjects inside that zone.

- **Use it for:** Moving subjects when face/eye isn't reliable—kids playing, runners, wildlife at moderate distance.

- **Avoid when:** You need pinpoint precision (macro, a subject behind branches). Use 1-Point/Expand instead.

1-Point AF (and Expand Area)

- **What it does:** A single point (with optional helpers around it).

- **Use it for:** Still subjects, backlit scenes, shooting through fences or glass, small subjects.

- **Avoid when:** Fast unpredictable motion—you'll chase with the point and lose frames.

If you only remember one pairing:

- Still subject → One-Shot + 1-Point (or Face/Eye if it locks).

- Moving subject → Servo + Face/Tracking or a small Zone.

AF MODES CHEAT SHEET

One-Shot AF	Servo AF	Manual Focus (MF)
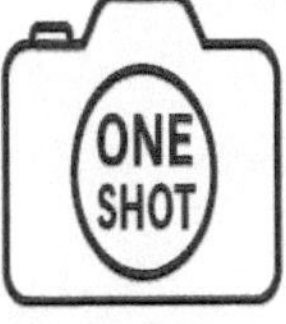	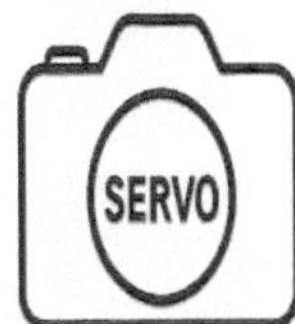	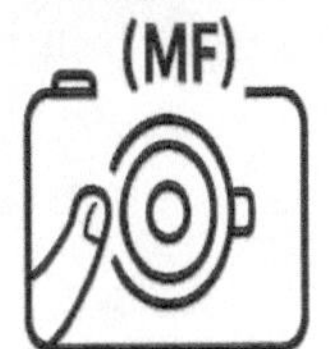
• Locks focus once when shutter is pressed halfway	• Continuously adjusts focus while shutter is pressed halfway	• You adjust focus by turning the focus ring
• Use it for: still subjects	• Use it for: moving subjects	• Use it for: situations AF may struggle (e.g., low light)
• Benefit: precise, allows recomposing after focus	• Benefit: tracks focus for each shot	• Benefit: full control over focus
• Watch out: not for moving subjects	• Watch out: needs a good subject to track	• Watch out: slower than autofocus

Eye and Face Detection — your best friend, with boundaries

Turn Eye Detection On for portraits, video interviews, family photos—any time a face is clear and fills a decent part of the frame. It's excellent.

Turn it Off (or just switch areas) when:

- Faces are tiny/far away.

- Your subject wears sunglasses, masks, or looks away for long stretches.

- There are multiple faces and the camera keeps choosing the wrong one.

- You're shooting macro or small objects where eyes don't exist.

Tip: if Eye AF can't catch, drop to Face + Tracking (without eye) or 1-Point / Zone and aim at contrasty edges: eyelashes, collar seams, a logo.

Back-button focus: small change, big upgrade

Assign focus to AF-ON and leave the shutter button for metering + shooting. Hold AF-ON to track in Servo; lift your thumb to stop updating focus. For One-Shot, tap AF-ON to lock focus, release, recompose, click. You'll get fewer accidental refocuses and more keepers.

Touch-and-drag AF: the missing joystick

When using the EVF, enable Touch & Drag AF so your thumb can slide the focus point on the rear screen like a trackpad. Set the active area to the right half of the screen if your nose hits the touchscreen. This makes selecting a point fast without taking your eye from the finder.

Real-world recipes (copy these, then tweak)

1) Single-person portrait, calm

- One-Shot, Face/Eye On. If it wobbles, switch to 1-Point and place it on the nearer eye.

- Open to f/2.8–f/4; keep shutter ≥ 1/125s (kids 1/250s).

- Add +0.3 to +0.7 EV if backlit.

2) Kids or pets running toward you

- **Servo + Face/Tracking** (or a small Zone if faces are tiny).

- Shutter 1/1000s outdoors, 1/500s if light is limited.

- If the AF jumps to the background, reduce tracking sensitivity a notch.

3) Street/travel with moving people

- **Servo** + Zone AF. Put the zone over your subject and follow; fire short bursts.

- Shutter 1/500s for pace; let Auto ISO handle the rest.

4) Wildlife behind branches / sports through a fence

- **Servo** + 1-Point **or** Expand Area. Aim through openings; keep the point glued to your subject.

5) Macro or tiny objects

- Manual Focus with peaking and 10× magnify.

- Rock your body slightly forward/back to refine focus; shoot a short burst.

6) Stage/event lighting

- **One-Shot** + **1-Point** aimed at a high-contrast edge (microphone, collar).

- Eye AF may struggle with heavy shadows—don't force it.

- Shutter ≥ 1/250s for performers; ISO will rise—okay.

7) Talking-head video

- Movie Servo AF On + Face/Eye On.

- If focus "breathes," slow AF speed/sensitivity for gentler pulls.

8) Product B-roll / controlled video rack

- Manual Focus, peaking On, magnify to set each rack.

- Practice a slow, confident pull; don't chase with AF.

Focus-and-recompose (when it's fine, when it's risky)

The classic move: lock focus in One-Shot, reframe, shoot. It's fine at f/4–f/8 or with subjects not super close.

It becomes risky at wide apertures (f/1.4–f/2.8) and close distances because the focus plane is thin; tilting the camera moves that plane off the eye. In those cases, move the AF point or use Eye AF.

Troubleshooting soft images (fix from fastest to deepest)

1. **Check where the AF point actually landed.** Review with focus point display enabled if you can. Did the box sit on the ear or background? Choose a smaller area or move the point.

2. **Raise shutter speed.** Many "AF problems" are motion blur. For people, stay at 1/125s minimum; for active scenes, 1/500–1/1000s.

3. **Stabilize yourself.** Elbows in, camera to your face, exhale and click. If you're on a tripod and the lens has IS, turn IS Off to avoid micro-jitter.

4. **Open or close the aperture appropriately.**

    o Too much of the frame soft? Stop down to f/5.6–f/8.

    o Background too distracting? Open up to f/2.8–f/4.

5. **Give AF a better target.** Aim at high-contrast edges (eye lashes, printed text, a jacket seam). In low light, add a tiny LED or move closer to window light.

6. **When AF hunts, go manual.** Turn the ring, use peaking and magnify. Get the shot, then troubleshoot later.

7. **Clean optics.** Smears on the front element or a cheap, dirty filter can soften everything. Quick blower + microfiber wipe.

8. **Set expectations with ISO/JPEG.** Very high ISO plus heavy in-camera noise reduction can make files look

"smudged." Shoot RAW/C-RAW if quality matters, or lower NR in-camera.

9. **Don't blame the EVF sharpness.** If the EVF text looks fuzzy, adjust the diopter; it's your eye, not the photo.

A fast mental flow when an image is soft: Did they move? Did I move? Where did the box land? Was depth of field too thin? Fix in that order.

A 60-second AF setup for two worlds

- **C1 — Portraits/Still:** One-Shot, Face/Eye On, 1-Point available on a button, f/2.8–f/4, shutter $\geq$1/125s.

- **C2 — Action:** Servo, Face/Tracking or small Zone, shutter 1/1000s, burst On, tracking sensitivity moderate.

Switching between C1 and C2 covers 90% of your life without menu diving.

AF AREA MODES

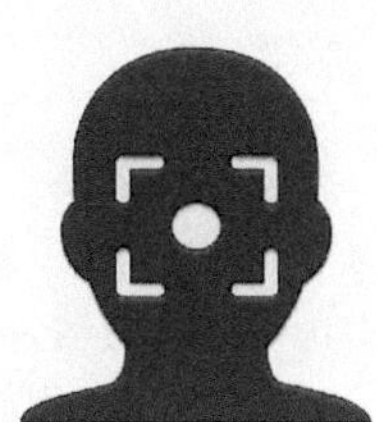

**FACE+
TRACKING**

- MOVING
  SUBJECTS

- FACE
  DETECTION

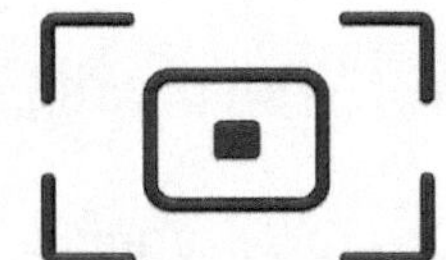

ZONE AF

- GROUPS OF
  SUBJECTS

- ACTION
  SHOTS

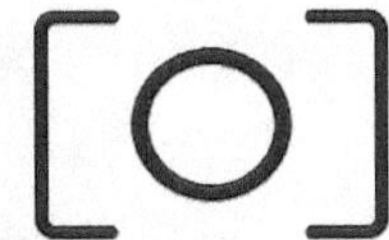

**1-POINT
AF**

- PRECISE
  FOCUS

- STILL
  SUBJECTS

Weekly two-minute drills

- **Drill 1 (precision):** Place the AF point on a small printed word across the room and take three frames at f/2.8. Check the letters at 100%.

- **Drill 2 (tracking):** Follow a jogger or a car with Servo + Zone, fire short bursts, and review which frames nailed the eyes/license plate.

- **Drill 3 (manual):** With peaking On, focus by hand on a coin at arm's length, then a second coin a little behind it—feel the plane of focus move.

Do these once a week, and your hit rate climbs fast.

Chapter 5

Unlocking the Power of Video

Flat color. Wobbly footage. Focus breathing in and out at the worst moments. None of that is you—it's your setup. Give the EOS R the right instructions and your video immediately looks intentional and confident. This chapter hands you a baseline that works anywhere, explains 4K vs. 1080p without jargon, makes frame rates second nature, and shows you how to keep focus steady while shooting handheld without a gimbal.

First principles (that matter more than specs)

- **Light** shapes everything. Window light at 45° beats mixed bulbs every time.

- **Sound** decides whether people keep watching. A tiny plug-in mic lifts perceived quality more than higher resolution.

- **Stability** equals trust. Hold each shot for five seconds, then move. The cut will feel calm.

Keep those three in your pocket while we set the camera.

Pick resolution for purpose; pick frame rate for feel.

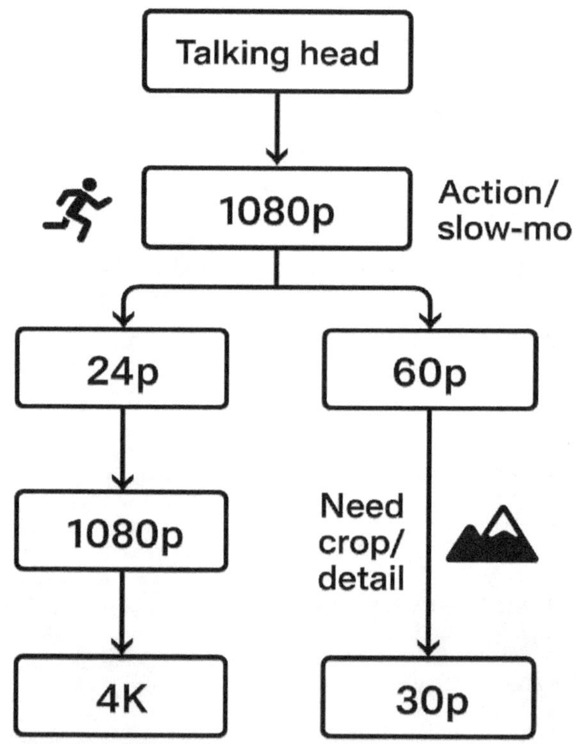

Pick resolution for purpose; pick frame rate for feel.

Best everyday video setups

1) YouTube talking head (clean, repeatable)

- **Resolution / fps:** 1080p at 24p for cinematic feel or 30p for a crisp look.

- **Shutter:** ~**1/50s** (24p) or **1/60s** (30p).

- **Aperture: f/2.8–f/4** for gentle background blur that doesn't breathe.

- **AF:** Movie Servo AF On, Face/Eye Detection On.

- **AF behavior:** Set AF speed slightly slower and tracking **sensitivity** toward Locked-On to prevent nervous pulsing.

- **WB:** Set and lock (don't leave Auto if the light is constant).

- **Audio:** External mic; Manual levels so peaks sit below clipping.

- **Stability:** Tripod or solid surface; Lens IS Off on a tripod to avoid micro-jitter.

2) Travel & street (detail + flexibility)

- **Resolution / fps:** 4K/30p for rich detail and cropping room or **1080p/60p** if you'll do gentle slow-motion.

- **Shutter:** ~1/60s (30p) or 1/125s (60p).

- **AF:** Movie Servo + Face/Tracking; zone AF if faces are small.

- **Stability:** Lens IS On; Digital IS Standard when walking; brace on doorways, railings, tables.

- **Tip:** Mix wide establishing shots with medium and detail shots; hold each at least five seconds.

3) Family moments (simple and forgiving)

- **Resolution / fps:** 1080p/30p (clean, small files).

- **Shutter:** ~1/60s.

- **Aperture:** f/2.8–f/4 indoors; f/4–f/5.6 outdoors.

- **AF:** Movie Servo + Face/Eye; tracking sensitivity one step more responsive for kids and pets.

- **Stability:** Keep elbows tucked; lean on a wall; short pans only.

Power tip for Nigeria/50Hz regions: Under mains-powered lights, pick 25p/50p and shutter around 1/50s/1/100s to minimize flicker. In 60Hz regions (e.g., US), 24/30/60p with 1/50/1/60/1/125 works well.

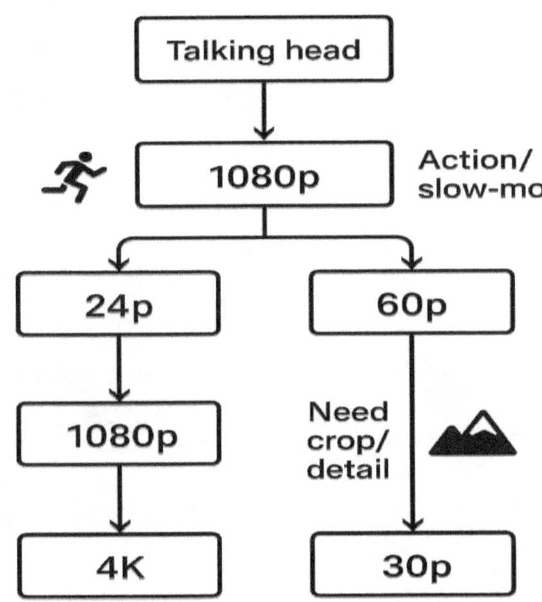

Pick resolution for purpose;
pick frame rate for feel.

4K vs. 1080p — when and why

Choose 4K when:

- You want extra detail and crop room in editing.

- You'll stabilize in post or pull still frames.

- You're shooting vistas, architecture, products, or anything with fine texture.

Choose 1080p when:

- You need smaller files, longer record times, and easier editing.

- You're capturing family, interviews, or quick social clips.

- You want 60p slow-motion without huge data rates.

A practical strategy: Capture 4K, deliver 1080p for premium sharpness and cropping flexibility—use it when you can manage the storage.

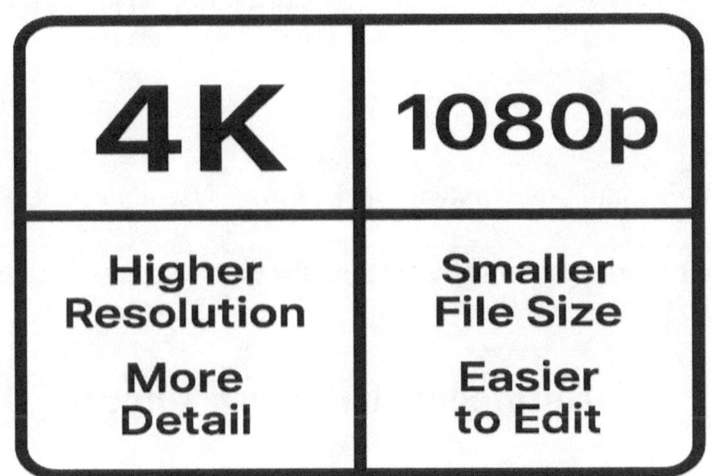

Frame rates in human words

- **24p:** Storytelling feel; a touch of motion blur; what movies use.

- **30p:** Clean, present, "TV" feel; great for YouTube and tutorials.

- **60p:** Smooth motion or half-speed slow-mo when you place it on a 30p/24p timeline.

The shutter rule (180° rule): set shutter close to 1 ÷ (2 × frame rate). 24p → ~1/50s; 30p → ~1/60s; 60p → ~1/125s. That keeps motion natural.

Bright day and your shutter's locked low? Use a variable ND filter to control brightness while keeping the shutter where it belongs.

Autofocus that doesn't hunt

- Use Face/Eye Detection for people, interviews, and vlogs.

- Slow the AF speed a notch and lower tracking sensitivity to avoid visible "breathing."

- Pre-focus and hold: tap AF-ON to confirm focus, then stop touching the controls while you speak or reframe slowly.

- Give it contrast: aim faces toward light; avoid deep backlight without fill.

- Switch to Zone or 1-Point when the face is small, turned, or blocked.

- Manual focus (with peaking and magnify) for product B-roll, macro, and deliberate rack-focus shots.

Smooth handheld without a gimbal

- **Stance:** feet staggered, elbows tucked, camera to the eye. Exhale, then move.

- **Moves:** slow pan, tilt, or a tiny push-in only; one movement per shot.

- **Walks:** heel-to-toe, bent knees; keep the camera close to your chest; let Digital IS Standard help.

- **Lens choice:** wider = steadier.

- **Support:** press a mini-tripod or strap against your body for a third point of contact.

- **Hold shots 5 seconds.** Editors (even future-you) need that tail.

- **Avoid "whip" reframes.** Stop recording, recompose, start again.

A tiny coverage plan that makes edits easy

For every scene, collect six short clips:

1. **Wide** (establish the place)

2. **Medium** (the action)

3. **Close-up** (hands, textures)

4. **Detail** (a single object)

5. **Push-in or pull-out** (gentle, slow)

6. **Cutaway** (something you can cut to: the sky, a sign, a reaction)

Hold each for ≥5 seconds. With just those six, you can build almost any one-minute sequence.

Quick troubleshooting

- **Focus "breathing" in and out:** Slow AF speed; lower tracking sensitivity; lock focus with AF-ON once composed.

- **Micro-jitter on a tripod:** Turn Lens IS Off and disable **Digital IS**.

- **Stutter under indoor lights:** Use 25p/50p (50Hz) or 30p/60p (60Hz) and matching shutters (1/50, 1/100 or 1/60, 1/120).

- **Overexposed outdoors with the shutter rule:** Add ND filter; don't crank shutter faster as a fix—you'll get choppy motion.

- **Harsh color shifts between clips:** Stop using Auto WB; set and lock a WB for the scene.

- **Hollow, echoey audio:** Move the mic closer (20–25 cm off-axis) and lift levels manually.

Three fast drills (do them once; remember forever)

1. **AF Confidence Drill**

   Record yourself at arm's length, then at 1.5 m, then at 3 m—each for 20 seconds. Face/Eye On, AF speed slow, tracking locked-on. Watch the eyes in playback. If it pulses, slow AF more.

2. **Stability Drill**

   Film a bookshelf or fence while panning slowly for five seconds, then tilting slowly, then a push-in from 1 m to 0.5 m. Review: it should feel like gliding, not drifting.

3. **Coverage Drill**

   In one room, capture the six-shot sequence (wide, medium, close-up, detail, push-in, cutaway). Drop them in order on a 30p timeline. You'll see how much story you can tell in 30–45 seconds.

You're ready

With these settings and habits, your EOS R will stop guessing and start obeying. The footage will look steadier, more flattering, and—most important—watchable. Next time you press record, think: *light, sound, stability*. Then let your settings do the heavy lifting.

MASTER QUICK GUIDE: EOS R ESSENTIALS

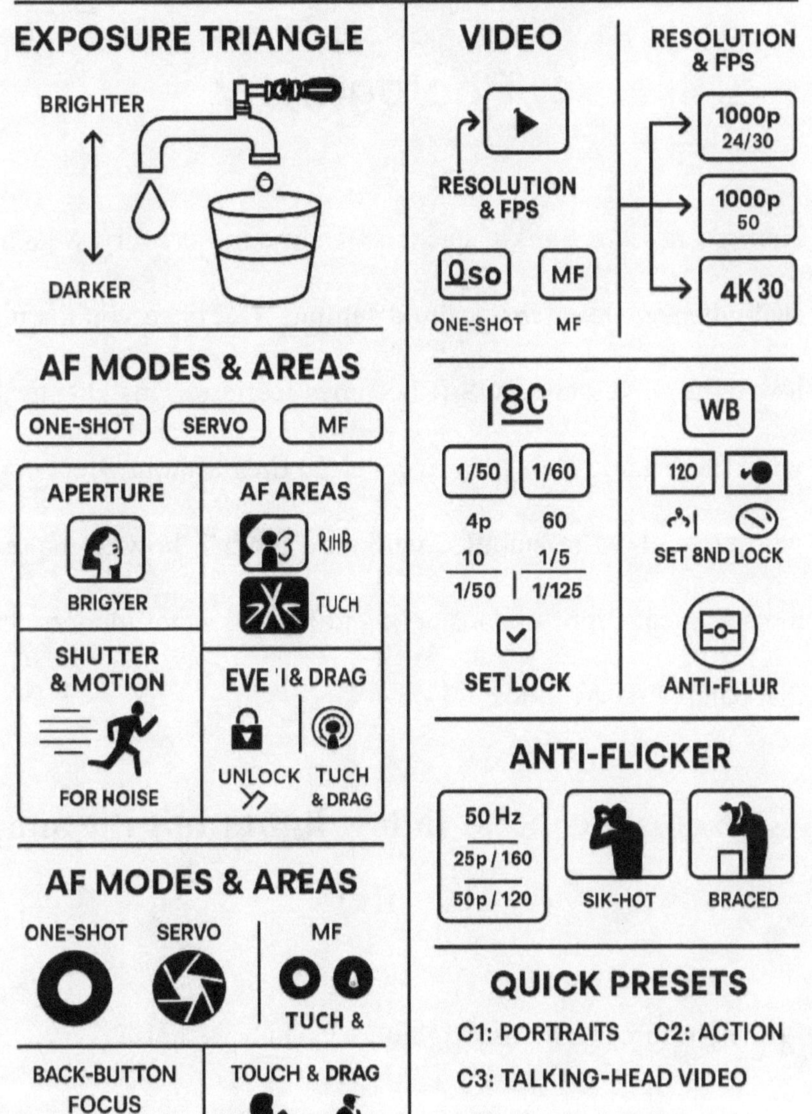

Chapter 6

Tackling Low-Light and Night Photography

Dark scenes are honest teachers. They expose every weakness—shaky hands, slow lenses, timid settings. But once you learn a few low-light moves, the EOS R becomes fearless. This chapter hands you a clear game plan: how to get clean files without wrecking them with noise, how to stabilize without a gimbal, how to make night look magical (light trails, stars), and how to shoot indoors without that harsh, "flashy" look.

The core problem in low light (and the simple fix)

Low light forces a trade: brightness vs. blur vs. noise.

- To make a photo brighter, you can open the aperture (smaller f-number), slow the shutter, **or** raise ISO.

- Each choice has a cost: wide aperture thins depth of field, slow shutter invites motion blur, high ISO adds grain.

Your job isn't to avoid the costs; it's to pay the right cost for the scene.

A quick decision flow you can trust:

1. **Is anything moving?** If yes, set a shutter that freezes it (people ≈ 1/125s, kids/pets 1/250s, sports 1/500–1/1000s**).**

2. **How much background blur do you want?** Open the aperture as needed (f/1.8–f/2.8 for portraits; f/4–f/5.6 for groups/rooms).

3. **Let ISO rise** to hit a good exposure (often ISO 1600–6400 in dim rooms).

4. If ISO climbs too high, add light (move closer to a window, turn on a lamp, bounce a flash) or stabilize for a slower shutter.

Best low-light defaults (that won't destroy image quality)

Mode: Av or Fv

- Av keeps the "look" in your hands; Fv lets you pin any one variable and leave the rest on Auto.

Aperture:

- People: f/1.8–f/2.8 if your lens allows (creamy background, more light).
- Groups/rooms: f/4–f/5.6 so more faces are sharp.

Shutter minimum (safety net):

- 1/125s for adults, 1/250s for kids/pets.
- If everyone's truly still, you can drop to 1/60s with good technique.

ISO:

- Auto ISO with a max of 6400 (clean enough on EOS R when exposed well).

- Expose a touch to the right (slightly brighter) to keep shadows clean, but protect highlights.

Metering / preview:

- Evaluative metering and Exposure Simulation ON in the EVF so you see what you'll get.

AF:

- Face/Eye Detection ON for people; switch to 1-Point on high-contrast edges if the camera hunts.

White Balance:

- Auto for mixed scenes; set Tungsten/Incandescent under warm bulbs for consistent skin tone. If you shoot RAW, WB is easy to fix later.

Faster lenses and stabilization (how they save the night)

Fast lenses (like f/1.8, f/1.4, f/2) are the biggest upgrade for low light.

- Moving from f/4 to f/2 is two stops more light—like turning ISO 6400 into ISO 1600 at the same shutter. That's the difference between "muddy" and "clean."

Image stabilization (IS) on RF lenses buys you 2–4 stops of hand-holdability on still subjects.

- If you can normally hand-hold sharply at 1/60s, IS might let you shoot at 1/15s without shake.
- IS does not freeze moving people; it only steadies *your* hands. Keep shutter fast enough for subject motion.

Handheld technique that actually works

- Feet staggered, elbows tucked, camera pressed to your face.

- Exhale, then click.

- Use a wall, table, doorframe—any third point of contact.

- Fire a short burst of 2–3 frames; often the middle frame is the sharpest.

Creative night techniques (make darkness look intentional)

1) City light trails (cars as paintbrushes)

- **Tripod** or firm support.

- **Mode:** M or Fv.

- **Shutter: 5–15s** to start (longer = longer trails).

- **Aperture: f/8–f/11** for crisp detail and star-burst streetlights.

- **ISO: 100–200** for clean files.

- **Focus:** Manual—pre-focus on a distant sign, use magnify to confirm.

- **Tip:** Trigger with the 2-sec timer or remote to avoid shake; watch highlights near bright signs—dial aperture or ISO accordingly.

2) Wide-angle night streets (handheld)

- **Lens:** wider = steadier (24–35 mm).

- **Shutter: 1/60–1/125s**; let ISO rise.

- **Aperture: f/2–f/2.8**.

- **ISO: 1600–6400**.

- **AF:** Zone or 1-Point on high-contrast edges.

- **Tip:** Use pools of light (shop windows, signs) as your "mini studios." Frame people as silhouettes crossing bright patches.

3) Stars / Milky Way (the simple recipe)

- **Tripod mandatory.** Turn off lens IS.

- **Lens:** the wider and faster, the better (14–24 mm, f/1.4–f/2.8).

- **Start settings:** 20s, f/2.8, ISO 3200. Adjust from there.

- **500 rule:** Max shutter (seconds) ≈ 500 / focal length (full-frame). At 24 mm, around 20s before stars smear.

- **Focus:** Manual: set near infinity, magnify a bright star, turn the ring until it's the smallest point.

- **WB:** 3500–4000 K for natural night color.

- **Tip:** Use Long Exposure NR only if you can tolerate slower shooting; otherwise, reduce noise in post.

4) Blue hour cityscapes (color + detail)

- **Timing:** 15–30 minutes after sunset, when the sky still glows.

- **Tripod:** yes.

- **Aperture: f/8**; **ISO 100**; shutter floats (often 1–8s).

- **Tip:** Arrive early, compose, and shoot as the light falls—each minute changes the mood.

Indoors without ugly flash (or with beautiful

flash)

You can get flattering indoor photos with no flash—or with flash that doesn't look like flash.

No-flash recipe (fast, natural):

- Move subjects near a window; turn faces slightly toward the light.

- Av, f/2–f/4, 1/125s minimum, Auto ISO up to 6400.

- Face/Eye AF ON.

- If skin looks dull against bright windows, add +0.3 to +0.7 EV.

Bounce-flash recipe (soft, invisible):

- On-camera flash aimed at a white ceiling or wall, not at faces.

- Angle about 45° up and 45° to the side; pull out the bounce card if available.

- TTL works well; dial Flash Exposure Compensation –0.3 to –1.0 for subtlety.

Gel the flash to match room light (slight CTO under warm bulbs); set WB accordingly so colors don't fight.

- Shutter: 1/125s (or your camera's sync speed).

- Aperture: f/2.8–f/4 for pleasing depth.

- **Tip:** Watch the direction of shadows—bounce off a wall to "fake" a window.

Continuous lights (easy alternative):

- A small LED panel through a white umbrella or bedsheet works wonders.

- Set WB to the light's Kelvin value so skin looks consistent.

Common low-light mistakes (and one-move

fixes)

- Everything is blurry: Your shutter is too slow. Raise it to 1/125s–1/250s for people, let ISO climb.

- Faces look orange/green: Set WB (Tungsten for warm bulbs; Daylight for window light) or shoot RAW and fix later.

- Grainy mush: You under-exposed. Add +0.3 to +0.7 EV, or add light, or use a faster lens.

- AF hunting: Aim at contrast (lashes, collar edge), switch to 1-Point, add more light, or go Manual + peaking.

- Tripod but still soft: Turn IS OFF on the lens; use 2-sec timer; avoid windy bridges and wobbly floors.

- Banding under bulbs: In Nigeria (50 Hz), use 1/50s or 1/100s; in 60 Hz regions, 1/60s or 1/120s.

Five quick drills to make low light second

nature

1. Shutter feel: Photograph a walking friend at 1/60, 1/125, 1/250. Learn exactly where motion freezes for you.

2. ISO tolerance: Same scene at ISO 800, 1600, 3200, 6400. Decide your personal limit (most are happy up to 6400 if exposed well).

3. Window portrait: One person, window at 45°. Shoot no-flash and bounce-flash versions. Compare skin and catchlights.

4. Handheld steadiness: With a 35 mm lens, test sharpness at 1/60, 1/30, 1/15 using good stance and IS. Keep the frame that surprises you.

5. Night creative: Make a 10-second light trail shot with tripod and timer. Then try blue hour at f/8, ISO 100. You'll feel the mood difference.

Your low-light checklist (pocket size)

- Choose shutter for motion, aperture for depth, let ISO rise.

- Use fast glass (f/1.8–f/2.8) whenever possible.

- Stabilize: elbows in, walls, tripods, short bursts.

- WB set (or RAW) to avoid weird color.

- For night looks: trails (5–15s), stars (20s, f/2.8, ISO 3200), blue hour (f/8, ISO 100).

- Indoors: window light or bounce flash—never bare flash to the face.

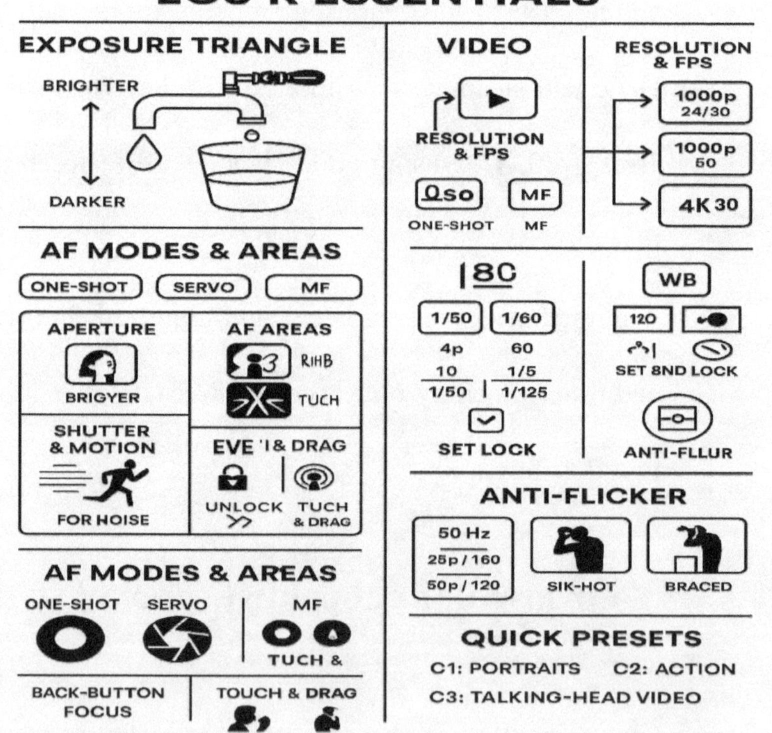

Chapter 7

Color, White Balance, and Creative Looks

When color feels wrong, everything feels wrong—skin looks sickly, rooms look dingy, sunsets look ordinary. The good news: accurate, flattering color is mostly a white balance problem, and white balance is easy to control once you know how the EOS R thinks. In this chapter you'll learn to set colors that stay consistent, choose picture styles that fit your taste, decide what to fix in-camera versus in editing, and use creative looks without turning your footage into a filter parade.

Color starts with light (and light has a color)

Every light source has a color temperature measured in Kelvin (K). Warm bulbs (indoor tungsten) are low on the scale and look orange;

daylight sits near the middle and looks neutral; shade can push cool/blue. Your camera isn't guessing "pretty"—it's trying to make the light neutral so whites look white and skin looks like skin. That correction is white balance (WB).

If you let the camera choose WB automatically, it often does well—but it can shift from shot to shot as the scene changes. If you want consistency, you set and lock it.

Setting white balance for accurate, repeatable color

Use Auto WB when the light changes (moving between indoors and outdoors, clouds racing overhead). It adapts quickly and keeps you shooting.

Lock WB when the light is steady (a living room, a studio, a cloudy day that won't change). Locking prevents subtle shifts that break the flow of a sequence.

Here are the practical ways to do it on the EOS R:

- **Presets**

  Daylight for sun, Shade when you're under trees or awnings, Cloudy on overcast days, Tungsten/Incandescent under warm indoor bulbs, and Fluorescent for office lighting. Presets keep a whole shoot consistent.

- **Kelvin (K) value**

  Dial a number when you want precision. Typical anchors: indoors around 3200 K (warm bulbs), daylight around 5200–5600 K, shade/cloudy around 6000–7500 K. Set it once and your colors won't drift.

- **Custom WB with a neutral target**

  Point the camera at a gray card (or a clean white card if that's what you have), fill the frame, take a photo, then set **Custom WB** using that frame. The camera measures the light in your room and nails it. This is the fastest route to natural skin.

- **AWB W (white priority) vs AWB A (ambience)**

  If your camera offers both, AWB W removes warmth for

truer white; AWB A leaves some cozy warmth. For events and homes, AWB A can be more flattering; for product shots, AWB W is safer.

Mixed light? Pick a hero. If window daylight battles orange lamp light, choose the look you care about most. Either turn off the competing source, move your subject deeper into one type of light, or gel your flash to match the room and set WB to that color. Trying to balance two different colors at once makes skin look strange.

Picture Styles vs. custom looks (what they do and don't do)

Picture Styles (Standard, Portrait, Neutral, etc.) change how your JPEGs (and your live preview) render contrast, color, and sharpening. If you're shooting RAW, the style doesn't bake into your data—but it does affect what you see in the EVF and on the back screen, which can influence exposure decisions. If you're shooting JPEG, Picture Style is the look you get.

- **Standard**: Balanced contrast and color—great default for most scenes.

- **Portrait**: Softer contrast and color tuned for skin; reduces harshness in faces.

- **Neutral**: Lower contrast/saturation; protects highlights and keeps colors gentle—excellent if you'll edit later.

- **Fine Detail**: Subtle sharpening and detail emphasis—good for textures and static scenes.

- **Monochrome**: In-camera black-and-white; you can also apply colored "filters" in-camera to shift how tones render.

You can tweak any style (contrast, saturation, color tone, sharpening) and save it as a User Def style. Small changes go a long way: a nudge of contrast, a touch less saturation for skin, a hair more sharpness for landscapes. Avoid extreme tweaks—you'll regret "Instagram-level" saturation on real skin.

For video, choose Standard if you won't grade, or Neutral (or your camera's flatter option) if you will. Flatter profiles hold more highlight detail but require color correction later. If you're not editing, don't choose flat—it will look dull out of camera.

In-camera color vs. editing later (what to decide where)

Do in camera:

- **White balance** when the light is constant. Locking WB keeps a series of photos or clips consistent and saves time later.

- **Picture Style choice** that matches your delivery: Standard/Portrait for ready-to-share, Neutral if you'll edit.

- **Avoid clipping highlights**—you can't fix blown white in post. Watch playback "blinkies" and nudge exposure down when needed.

Do later (editing):

- **Fine-tune WB** (especially in RAW). One click on a gray area can fix an entire batch.

- **Match shots** (copy color settings from one keeper across a whole scene).

- **Tasteful contrast and saturation**—subtle global changes beat heavy in-camera processing.

- **Skin tone finesse** (light HSL adjustments) if a room tint persists.

A simple policy: Nail the white balance and exposure in camera; enjoy the polish in post. That combo keeps you fast on the day and consistent afterward.

Creative looks without overdoing them

Creative looks should serve the story, not drown it. Use them like seasoning.

- **Monochrome with intent**

  Black-and-white can save a mixed-light disaster or focus

attention on expression and shape. In-camera Monochrome is lovely—add a subtle yellow or orange "filter" in-camera to lift skin and deepen skies. Keep contrast modest; let faces breathe.

- **Warmth for coziness**

In homes and restaurants, a touch of warmth feels right. Use AWB (ambience) or set Kelvin around 4000–4500 K to leave some golden glow without going orange.

- **Cool for night mood**

For night streets or techy vibes, push Kelvin lower (e.g., 3200–3600 K) to let blue tones through. Set it deliberately so it's consistent across the sequence.

- **Vivid/detail looks for scenery**

For landscapes and architecture, a mild boost in saturation and sharpness can help detail pop. Avoid pushing reds—skin and brick can turn cartoonish fast.

- **HDR and special effects**

In-camera HDR and effects can be fun, but they're easy to

spot. If a look screams "filter," pull back. When in doubt, shoot a clean version and a creative one so you have options later.

The rule of thumb: if the look calls attention to itself, it's too strong. People should notice the subject, not the settings.

Real-world recipes you can copy

Portraits near a window (natural skin)

Lock WB to Daylight or Kelvin 5200–5600 K. Picture Style Portrait or Neutral. Add +0.3 EV if the face is against a bright background. If the room is warm and you love the vibe, choose Kelvin 4500 K to keep just a hint of warmth in the skin.

Indoor evening with warm bulbs (consistent color)

Turn off extra lamps of different colors. Set Kelvin ≈ 3200–3400 K or use Tungsten preset. Picture Style Standard or Portrait. If it still feels a touch green (some fluorescents), nudge WB Shift toward magenta a step or two.

Travel streets at blue hour (mood without mud)

Lock Kelvin ≈ 6000–6500 K to keep the sky rich and shop lights warm. Picture Style Neutral to protect highlights, then add gentle contrast in editing.

Product or food (true color)

Use a gray card for Custom WB; set Picture Style Neutral with a hair more sharpness. Keep color clean in-camera; add micro-contrast later.

Video interviews (no color drift)

Lock WB to a specific Kelvin for the key light (e.g., 5600 K for daylight, 3200 K for tungsten). Don't leave Auto WB on—tiny shifts between takes are obvious. Picture Style Standard if you'll deliver straight away, Neutral if you'll grade.

Troubleshooting weird color—fast fixes

- Faces look too orange indoors: Lower Kelvin toward 3000–3400 K or switch to Tungsten.

- Everything looks blue in shade: Raise Kelvin toward 6500–7500 K or use Shade preset.

- Green cast under office lights: Use Fluorescent preset; if needed, add a magenta WB shift by one or two steps.

- Colors change between shots in the same room: You used Auto WB. Lock Kelvin or Custom WB and reshoot the set.

- Skin is oversaturated: Choose Portrait style or reduce saturation one notch; expose slightly to the right and bring contrast back later.

- Video clips don't match: One was Auto WB, one was fixed—pick one approach. For interviews, always lock white balance.

Simple practice to make color second nature

- **Ten-minute WB walk:** Photograph the same white sheet under daylight, shade, and a lamp. Set Daylight, then Shade, then Tungsten, then Kelvin manually to match each. You'll feel the difference immediately.

- **Custom WB quick-draw:** Keep a small gray card in your bag. In a new room, set a custom WB in thirty seconds. Watch how skin tones settle.

- **Portrait portrait:** Shoot one portrait at AWB, one at Kelvin 5200 K, one at Portrait style, one at Neutral. Compare. Decide your favorite baseline and save it as a Custom Mode.

Pocket checklist

- If the light is steady, lock WB (Kelvin or Custom).

- If the light changes, use Auto WB and focus on moments.

- Pick a Picture Style that suits delivery: Standard/Portrait for ready-to-share, Neutral for editing.

- Don't chase mixed light—choose a hero light or match your flash to the room.

- Creative looks are seasoning, not the meal.

Chapter 8

Lenses and Accessories That Actually Help

Gear is supposed to make your life easier, not drain your wallet. This chapter is a calm buyer's guide: which lenses will immediately improve your photos and video, what to skip for now, and which accessories pull the most weight per naira. You'll finish with a lean kit that covers portraits, landscapes, and video without regret purchases.

The simple way to think about lenses

Focal length changes what fits in the frame and how a scene feels:

- Wide (14–24 mm): Fits more in; makes spaces feel larger; exaggerates lines—great for landscapes, interiors, and dramatic perspective.

- Normal (35–50 mm): Feels natural, like what your eyes
  see; fantastic for everyday storytelling and portraits in tight
  spaces.

- Short telephoto (85–135 mm): Compresses background;
  flattering portraits; isolates subjects outdoors.

Aperture controls light and background blur. Lenses that open
wide (f/1.8, f/2) are called fast—they keep ISO lower in dim rooms
and give you creamy bokeh.

On the EOS R, RF lenses are native. You can also adapt EF lenses
with a simple adapter—they're often cheaper on the used market
and still perform beautifully.

Must-have first lenses (portrait, landscape,

video)

Portraits (choose one to start)

- **50 mm f/1.8:** The classic. Inexpensive, light, flattering for single-person portraits, and bright enough for indoor window light. You'll learn composition and timing without wrestling your budget.

- **85 mm f/2 (with close-focus):** More background blur and "compression." Perfect outdoors or in bigger rooms; the closer focusing is a bonus for details like hands, rings, or flowers.

- **35 mm f/1.8 (often with macro + IS):** Unbeatable for small spaces and environmental portraits. The built-in stabilization helps for handheld stills and video.

How to pick: If you shoot mostly indoors or travel light, start with 35 mm f/1.8. If you want classic head-and-shoulders portraits with creamy backgrounds, choose 50/1.8 on a budget or 85/f2 if you have room to step back.

Landscapes (one lens that opens the world)

- **Wide zoom in the 14–35 mm or 16–35 mm range:** Lets you work foregrounds (rocks, rails, flowers) against big skies.

- **24–105 mm walkaround zoom (f/4 or f/4–7.1):** Versatile travel lens; covers wide scenes, portraits, and details in one. Pair this with a small prime and you can shoot almost anything.

How to pick: If landscapes/interiors are your thing, go ultra-wide zoom first. If you want one lens for trips and family days, 24–105 is the stress-free choice.

- **24–70 mm (f/2.8 or f/4):** Bread-and-butter for talking heads, B-roll, and events. One twist covers wide, medium, and tight shots.

- **35 mm f/1.8 with IS:** A dream for handheld walk-and-talks and product B-roll; bright, light, stabilized.

- **16–18 mm prime or wide zoom:** For vlogging and tight spaces where you need arm's-length framing.

Bonus for video: Add a variable ND filter so you can keep your shutter near the 180° rule (≈1/50s at 24p; ≈1/60s at 30p) even in bright sun.

Budget-friendly buying (without regret)

- **Start with one zoom + one prime.** A 24–105 (or your kit zoom) plus a fast 35 or 50 covers 90% of real life. Learn them deeply before you add more.

- **Buy used from reputable sellers.** Lenses hold value. Inspect for smooth focus/zoom, clean glass (minor dust is fine), no fungus or haze, and responsive autofocus.

- **Rent before you leap.** If you're eyeing a specialty lens (ultra-wide, 70–200, macro), rent it for a weekend to see if it fits your style.

- **Avoid overlap for the sake of it.** If you own a 24–105, you probably don't need a 24–70 immediately—spend on a fast prime instead.

- **Choose stabilization when it matters.** If you shoot a lot of handheld video, prefer lenses with **IS**; it makes footage calmer without a gimbal.

- **Filter smart:** Buy one larger-diameter quality filter (like 67 or 77 mm) and a set of step-up rings to use it across lenses. It's cheaper and you carry less.

- **Skip the halo of cheap accessories.** Bargain variable NDs, flimsy tripods, and random "UV protectors" can worsen image quality more than they protect anything.

Accessories worth buying (in this order)

1) A tripod you'll actually use

- **Travel tripod (light, folds small):** Perfect for city night shots, self-portraits, and time-lapses.

- **Full-size tripod (sturdy):** For long exposures, landscapes in wind, and precision work.

- **Ball head with a quick-release plate:** Faster than fiddly handles.

  Tips: Don't extend the center column unless you must; use the 2-second timer or a remote to avoid shake.

2) Microphones that fix "video that feels amateur"

- **On-camera shotgun mic:** Clearer ambient sound; great for run-and-gun clips.

- **Lavalier mic (wired or wireless):** Clean voice for talking heads and tutorials.

Set levels manually so peaks sit below clipping, and monitor with headphones when you can.

3) Small, soft light that flatters faces

- **Bi-color LED panel** with a soft diffuser (or bounce it off a wall/ceiling).

- **Reflector or a sheet of white card** to lift shadows under eyes.

  Rule: Bigger light = softer light. Move it closer rather than blasting brightness.

4) Filters that actually help

- **Variable ND (quality):** Essential for outdoor video to keep motion natural. Look for smooth rotation with minimal color shift.

- **Circular Polarizer (CPL):** Cuts glare on water/leaves and deepens skies—landscape staple.

- **Skip most "special effects" filters** until you have a reason.

5) Power and storage

- **Two extra batteries** for a full shooting day.

- **Fast SD cards** rated U3/V30 (or higher) for reliable video and bursts.

- **Card reader + external SSD** for backups on travel.

6) Smart supports for real life

- **Wrist strap or comfy neck strap** you'll actually wear.

- **Mini tripod or clamp** for low angles and table-top video.

- **Lens hood** (often included with higher-end lenses): real flare protection and a little bump-guard.

Essential cleaning and maintenance

- Rocket blower: Your first move for dust—sensor and lenses.

- Microfiber cloths + a drop of lens solution: For smudges; wipe in gentle circles from center outward.

- Lens brush / pen: For dry particles on glass edges.

- Sensor care: Use the camera's automatic sensor clean first. If you still see spots, try a blower with the camera in sensor cleaning mode. Only wet-clean with the proper swabs if you're confident; otherwise, use a pro service annually or when needed.

- Storage: Keep lenses capped, dry, and ventilated. A small silica gel pack in your bag or cabinet helps in humid climates.

- Firmware updates: Check periodically; updates can improve AF and stability.

What to skip (for now)

- **Huge gimbals** if you're not filming cinematic moves; learn stable handheld technique first.

- **A bag of overlapping primes** when one or two cover your needs.

- **Ultralong telephotos** if you don't shoot wildlife or sports— they're expensive, heavy, and rarely used by beginners.

- **Ultra-cheap tripods/filters.** Shaky legs and color-shifting glass will hurt your footage more than help.

Starter kits for real people

- **The two-lens starter:** 24–105 zoom + 50/1.8. You'll stop making excuses and start making work.

- **The storyteller set:** 35/1.8 (with IS) + 85/f2. Indoors, outdoors, portraits, and detail—done.

- **The video-first kit:** 24–70 (f/2.8 or f/4) + variable ND + on-camera mic + small LED. Clean, stable, and watchable from day one.

Build slowly. Every new piece should unlock a shot you truly want—not just fill a spot in a bag.

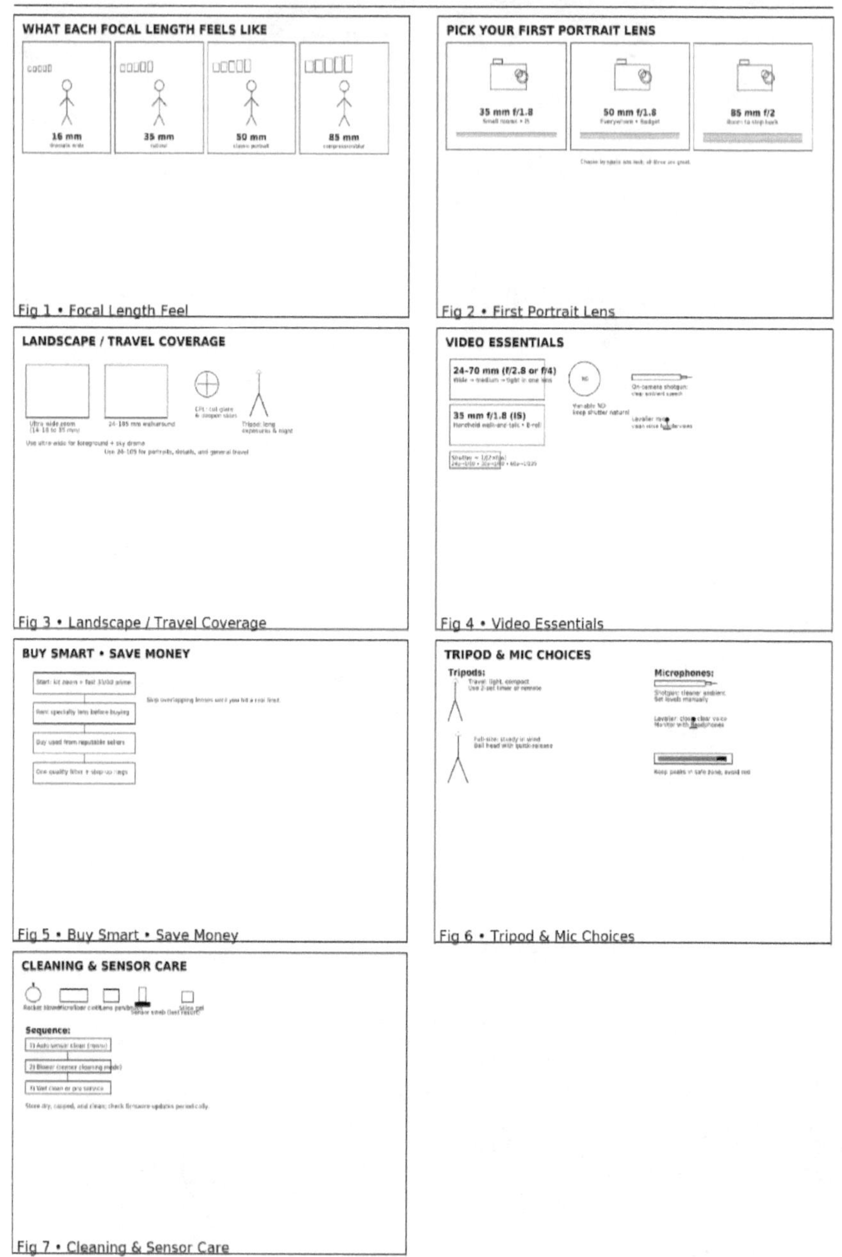

Fig 1 • Focal Length Feel

Fig 2 • First Portrait Lens

Fig 3 • Landscape / Travel Coverage

Fig 4 • Video Essentials

Fig 5 • Buy Smart • Save Money

Fig 6 • Tripod & Mic Choices

Fig 7 • Cleaning & Sensor Care

Chapter 9

Real-Life Shooting Scenarios

Theory is the map; real life is the road. This chapter gives you copy-and-shoot setups for common situations so you can get great results without second-guessing. Each recipe includes lens choice, core settings, a quick shot list, and "if it's going wrong" fixes. No fluff—just what to do, in order.

Family Portraits (indoors + outdoors)

What to bring

- Lens: 35mm f/1.8 (small rooms) or 50mm f/1.8 (general use). Outside with space, 85mm f/2 is gorgeous.

- Optional: reflector/white card, small on-camera flash for bounce.

Setup (indoors)

1. Put your subject near a window; turn faces 45° toward the light.

2. Kill mixed light: turn off other odd-colored lamps.

3. Hold a white card on the shadow side to lift the cheeks/eyes.

Setup (outdoors)

1. Shoot golden hour or open shade.

2. Backlight hair with the sun; expose for faces and let the background glow.

Camera settings

- **Mode:** Av.

- **Aperture:** f/2–f/2.8 (single) or f/3.5–f/5.6 (two+ people).

- **Shutter floor:** 1/125s (adults), 1/250s (kids).

- **ISO:** Auto, max 3200–6400.

- **AF:** One-Shot + Face/Eye; if it wobbles, switch to 1-Point on the nearer eye.

- **WB: Daylight** by a window / Kelvin 5500–6000K outside for consistency.

Shot list (fast)

- Hero (waist-up), tight headshot, full length, siblings together, parents with each child, details (hands, hair), candid laugh.

If it's going wrong

- Busy background? Open aperture (lower f-number) and step closer.

- Kids won't hold still? Switch to Servo, 1/500s, burst short bursts.

- Flat skin tones? Turn faces a touch more toward the light or bounce a bit of white.

Travel & Street

What to bring

- Lens: 24–105mm walkaround or a 35mm f/1.8 for light, discreet shooting.

- Optional: CPL (glare control), tiny LED for food/objects.

Setup

1. Think three layers: foreground, subject, background (signs, frames, reflections).

2. Work the scene: wide → medium → close at every stop.

Camera settings

- **Mode:** Fv (pin shutter + aperture), or Tv if you want to lock motion.

- **Shutter:** 1/500s for people in motion; 1/1000s for bikes/cars.

- **Aperture:** f/4–f/5.6 (depth + speed).

- **ISO:** Auto; don't fear ISO 3200 at night if you expose well.

- **AF:** Servo + Zone (or Face/Tracking when a face fills the frame).

- **WB:** Auto in mixed light; Kelvin if you want a consistent mood.

Shot list

- Establishing place (wide), human moment (mid), detail (close), sign/texture, reflection (glass/puddle), food/market still life.

If it's going wrong

- Missed focus while walking? Raise shutter to 1/500–1/1000s, keep Servo + Zone, and brace the camera to your face.

- Banding under bulbs? Use 1/50s/1/100s (50Hz regions) or 1/60s/1/120s (60Hz).

Action Sports

What to bring

- Lens: 70–200mm if available; otherwise 24–105 and get closer. Indoors/low light, a fast 85/1.8 can save you.

Setup

1. Find a predictable spot (finish line, apex of a turn, jump).

2. Stand where backgrounds are clean and faces/jerseys are visible.

Camera settings

- **Mode:** M or Tv.

- **Shutter:** 1/1000s (outdoor daylight), 1/500s (indoor court), 1/30–1/60s for pans (intentional motion blur).

- **Aperture:** as open as you can in poor light (f/2–f/2.8 fast primes; f/4 zooms).

- **ISO:** Auto; cap around 6400 and expose a touch bright.

- **AF:** Servo, small Zone; Back-button focus on AF-ON.

- **Drive:** High-speed continuous.

- **Tracking sensitivity:** a notch toward Locked-On to avoid jumping.

Shot list

- Face-on run/jump, side profile at peak action, celebration/reaction, detail (hands on ball/bike), wide context (crowd + field).

If it's going wrong

- Soft results? It's probably motion blur—raise shutter first.

- AF jumping to background? Use a smaller AF area and keep the box glued to the torso/helmet.

- Indoors flicker? Match fps/shutter to mains frequency or enable anti-flicker.

Wildlife

What to bring

- Lens: the longest you have. 300–400mm+ is ideal; if not, get closer and wait.

- Optional: monopod/tripod, camouflage/neutral clothing, remote.

Setup

1. Arrive early, pick a good background (clean, distant), and stay still.

2. Watch patterns: perches, paths, feeding spots.

Camera settings

- **Mode:** M or Tv.

- **Shutter**: 1/1000s for birds; 1/500s for larger mammals.

- **Aperture:** wide open (f/4–f/6.3) for separation.

- **ISO:** Auto; don't fear ISO 6400 for birds at dawn—better sharp and grainy than soft.

- **AF:** Servo + small Zone; avoid full-frame tracking if the subject is tiny in frame.

- **Drive:** High-speed; shoot short bursts when the head turns toward you.

- **Stabilization:** On for handheld; off on tripod.

Shot list

- Profile in clean light, behavior (preen/hunt), environmental wide, tight eye contact, take-off/landing.

If it's going wrong

- Heat shimmer softening images? Shoot when air is cooler (early/late), shorten the distance, or raise up to reduce heat waves.

- AF grabs foreground branches? Switch to 1-Point/Expand and aim through gaps.

- Skittish subjects? Stay low, move slow, and wait. Patience beats chasing.

Product Photography (home setup)

What to bring

- Lens: 50mm f/1.8 or 35mm macro/1:2.

- Tripod, white board (sweep), window as key light, white/black cards for fill/contrast. Optional CPL for glassy objects.

Setup (window light)

1. Place a table by a window; tape a sheet of white paper to create a curved background (seamless).

2. Put the product about 30–60 cm from the background; side-light from the window; add a white card opposite to fill shadows.

Camera settings

- **Mode:** M.

- **Aperture:** f/5.6–f/11 (front-to-back sharpness).

- **Shutter:** whatever the meter needs on a tripod (don't worry if it's slow).

- **ISO:** 100–200.

- **AF:** One-Shot, 1-Point on a logo/edge; use magnify to verify.

- **WB: Kelvin** to match light (e.g., 5600K daylight) or **Custom WB** with a gray card.

Special cases

- **Shiny objects:** Use a CPL to tame glare; enlarge the white **card** so reflections look like soft windows.

- **Tiny items:** Consider focus stacking—shoot a series from front to back at f/5.6 and blend in software.

- Hero (straight-on), angled three-quarter, detail close-up, scale reference (hand/coin), packaging.

If it's going wrong

- Background looks gray? Bring the product forward and overexpose the sweep by +0.3 to +1.0 EV.

- Edges look jagged? Use f/8–f/11, tripod, and 2-sec timer to eliminate shake.

A 60-Second Cheat Routine (any scenario)

1. Light: Which direction? Is it steady? (If steady, lock WB.)

2. Motion: Freeze or blur? Set shutter for that first.

3. Look: Choose aperture for depth.

4. ISO: Let it rise to match exposure; avoid underexposing.

5. AF area: Small for precision, Zone/Face for moving people.

6. Stability: Brace, breathe, 2-sec timer on tripod; short bursts handheld.

7. Coverage: Wide → medium → close → detail → context → candid.

Do this in order and you'll spend less time fiddling, more time shooting—and your photos will look like you meant them to.

Family Portraits

Do: Window light • faces 45° to light • switch off mixed bulbs
Dial: Av • f/2-f/2.8 (single) / f/4-f/5.6 (groups) • 1/125–1/250s • Auto ISO
AF: Face/Eye; switch to 1-Point on nearer eye if it hunts
Fix: Busy bg → open aperture + step closer • Kids → Servo + 1/500s

Travel & Street

Do: Layers — Foreground → Subject → Background; WIDE → MEDIUM
Dial: Fv/Tv • 1/500-1/1000s • f/4-f/5.6 • Auto ISO • AWB
AF: Servo + Zone; Face/Tracking when a face fills the frame
Fix: Walking blur → 1/1000s + brace • Harsh light → open shade

Action Sports

ND Filter

Do: Predictable spot (finish line/apex). Clean background.
Dial: M/Tv • 1/1000s daylight • 1/500s indoor • 1/30–1/60s pans • Auto ISO
AF: Servo • small Zone • AF-ON • High-speed drive
Fix: Soft → faster shutter • AF jumps → smaller AF + Locked-On

Wildlife

Do: Arrive early; stay still; distant, uncluttered backgrounds.
Dial: M/Tv • 1/1000s birds • 1/500s mammals • f/4-f/6.3 • Auto ISO
AF: Servo + small Zone • High-speed bursts • IS On handheld
Fix: Heat shimmer → early/late • Branches → 1-Point/Expand

Product Photography

Do: Table by window; curved white sweep; white card fill.
Dial: M • f/5.6-f/11 • ISO 100-200 • Shutter floats on tripod
WB/AF: Kelvin ~5600K or Custom • 1-Point AF + magnify
Fix: Gray bg → +0.3-+1.0EV • Shiny → CPL + bigger white card

60-Second Routine

1) Light steady? Lock WB (Kelvin/Custom).

2) Motion goal? Set shutter first.

3) Depth look? Pick aperture.

4) ISO up to match exposure—avoid underexposing.

5) AF area: small for precision; Zone/Face for moving people.

6) Stability: brace; 2-sec timer on tripod; short bursts handheld.

7) Coverage: Wide → Medium → Close → Detail → Context → Candid.

Chapter 10

Common Problems & Quick Fixes

You don't need a weekend lost in forums to fix the basics. Use these quick, camera-in-hand checklists. They're written for the Canon EOS R, but most ideas carry across the RF system.

1) Camera won't turn on

Fast checks (in order):

- Battery: Charge fully; reseat it until you feel the spring catch. Try a known-good battery if you have one.

- Doors & switches: Close the battery door and card door firmly (the EOS R won't power on if either switch isn't closed). Confirm the power switch is actually ON.

- Memory card: Remove the card and try to power on. A faulty card can halt startup. If it boots without a card, format that card in-camera or replace it.

- Lens mount: Remove and reattach the lens; check that electrical contacts on lens and mount are clean and shiny (use a dry microfiber—no liquids).

- Cables/accessories: Unplug HDMI/USB, remove remote triggers, grips, or cages that could press buttons or short a port.

- Freeze reset: Take out the battery, wait 30 seconds, reinsert and power on.

If still dead:

Test with another battery and another card. If it still won't power, that's a service case.

2) Can't connect to phone/Wi-Fi

Start clean (this solves most pairing headaches):

1. On the EOS R: MENU → Setup (wrench) → Wireless communication settings.

2. Choose Wi-Fi and Bluetooth: set Disable, then Clear settings (look for "Reset/clear communication settings" or "Erase Wi-Fi settings.").

3. Re-enable Bluetooth first; then Wi-Fi.

Fresh pairing to Canon Camera Connect (recommended path):

- On the camera: MENU → Wireless communication settings → Bluetooth function → Pairing.

- In the app: add a new camera and follow prompts. The phone will use Bluetooth to establish a low-power link, then the camera will hand off to Wi-Fi when needed.

If it still won't connect:

- Forget the camera in your phone's Bluetooth/Wi-Fi settings, then re-pair.

- Use 2.4 GHz Wi-Fi (the EOS R doesn't do 5 GHz). Avoid hotel/captive networks.

- Toggle Airplane mode OFF on the camera (if you've used it to save battery).

- Update the Canon Camera Connect app and check for camera firmware updates.

- Stand away from heavy interference (routers crammed together, metal racks).

- For direct Wi-Fi transfer, choose Camera access point mode (the camera creates its own network) instead of trying to join a complex home network.

3) Overheating or thermal warnings (mostly video)

What's normal: Long high-bitrate recording builds heat. A temperature icon or auto-stop protects the camera.

Practical heat management:

- Dial down the load: If you're recording in 4K and don't need it, switch to 1080p. If you need 4K, use lower frame rates and IPB compression instead of ALL-I to reduce data rate.

- Short takes: Record in shorter clips (5–10 minutes), give the camera a minute between takes.

- Vent the body: Flip the rear LCD away from the camera and avoid pressing it flat to the body—it traps heat.

- Environment: Shade the camera; avoid parked-car dashboards and direct midday sun.

- Stabilization features: If you don't need Digital IS for video, turn it OFF—processing adds heat.

- External help (effective): Feed clean HDMI to an external recorder/monitor. The camera does less internal encoding, which can significantly cut heat buildup.

- Power choice: A dummy battery/AC adapter can reduce heat from battery discharge inside the body.

If it overheats anyway: Power off, open the card/battery doors for airflow, and cool the camera (shade or a small fan). Resume with lower load settings.

4) Battery draining too fast

The big drains and how to tame them:

- Screen/EVF time: Set Auto power off to 1 min (or less) and reduce LCD brightness a notch.

- Wireless radios: Disable Wi-Fi/Bluetooth when you don't need remote control or geotagging.

- Continuous AF & metering: If you don't need it, turn Servo AF off for still subjects and shorten the Metering timer.

- Lens IS: Optical stabilization in the lens uses power. Keep IS ON for handheld, OFF on a tripod.

- Review habits: Turn Image review down to 2 sec (or off) and chimp less.

- Cold weather: Keep batteries warm in a pocket; swap and rotate. Lithium cells dip hard in the cold.

Smart carries:

- Two spare batteries, a USB-C power bank + PD dummy battery, and a dual charger so you're never waiting on one brick.

5) Resetting settings safely (without losing your mind)

Before you reset anything:

- Snapshot your setup: Take phone photos of key menus (AF, custom buttons, exposure, video). It's faster than notes.
- Save your look: If you rely on particular combos, register them to C1/C2/C3 as custom modes (still shooting) so you can restore quickly.

- Backup to card (if available): Some EOS R menus include "Save/load settings on card." If you see it under the Setup (wrench) tabs, use it.

A safe reset order (least destructive first):

1. Clear communication settings (Wi-Fi/Bluetooth).

2. Clear custom functions / customized buttons.

3. Reset camera settings (shooting + setup).

4. Re-enter date/time and basic preferences, then rebuild only what you truly use.

After a reset:

Test AF method, image quality (RAW/JPEG), and your back-button AF preference—the three most commonly forgotten tweaks.

6) Blurry photos

Blurry breaks down into three root causes. Diagnose it once; fix it forever.

A) Camera shake (your hands moved)

How it looks: Everything in the frame is smeared in the same direction.

Fix it:

- Use the 1 / focal length rule on full frame, then give yourself margin: at 50 mm, try 1/100s (or faster). High-res sensors are less forgiving.

- Raise ISO so the camera can keep the shutter fast.

- Stabilize: Use a wall, table, strap tension, or a tripod/mini tripod. Fire with the 2-sec timer or a remote.

- On a tripod, turn IS OFF (lens) to prevent micro-jitters.

B) Subject motion (they moved)

How it looks: Background is sharp, the person or object streaks.

Fix it:

- Shutter speed: People walking 1/250s; kids/sports 1/500–1/1000s; birds in flight 1/1000s+.

- AF mode: Switch to Servo (continuous). Use Zone AF or Face/Eye for people; keep the AF box on the torso/face.

- Shoot short bursts at peak action; you'll get a tack-sharp frame in each burst.

C) Missed focus (AF locked on the wrong thing)

How it looks: Some other object is razor sharp; eyes aren't.

Fix it:

- AF area: For precise portraits, use 1-Point AF on the nearer eye. For moving people, use Face/Eye with Servo. For small/distant subjects (wildlife), use a small Zone and avoid full-frame tracking.

- Contrast & light: AF works best with texture and light. Add a little light, turn the face slightly toward the window, or focus on an edge (eyelash, collar).

- Lens switch: Make sure the lens is set to AF, not MF.

- Clean contacts: If AF hunts or fails, reseat the lens and wipe contacts with a dry microfiber.

Pro tip to diagnose:

Zoom to 100% in playback (tap INFO to show shutter speed/ISO). If the eyes are soft at 1/50s on a 50 mm lens, that's camera shake. If hands/feet smear but the background's crisp, that's subject motion. If the ear is sharp instead of the eye, that's missed focus. Different cause, different cure.

When in doubt: the 30-second rescue drill

1. Set Av, f/4, Auto ISO (cap 6400).

2. Set Minimum shutter (Safety: 1/250s) in the ISO speed settings, or switch to Tv 1/500s for fast action.

3. AF: Face/Eye + Servo for people; 1-Point for still objects.

4. WB: Auto for mixed light; Kelvin/Daylight if the light is steady.

5. If it's still not right, bump ISO one stop and shutter one stop—sharp first, noise second.

Breathe. The camera wants to help. These moves tell it exactly how.

CHAPTER 10 — COMMON PROBLEMS & QUICK FIXES

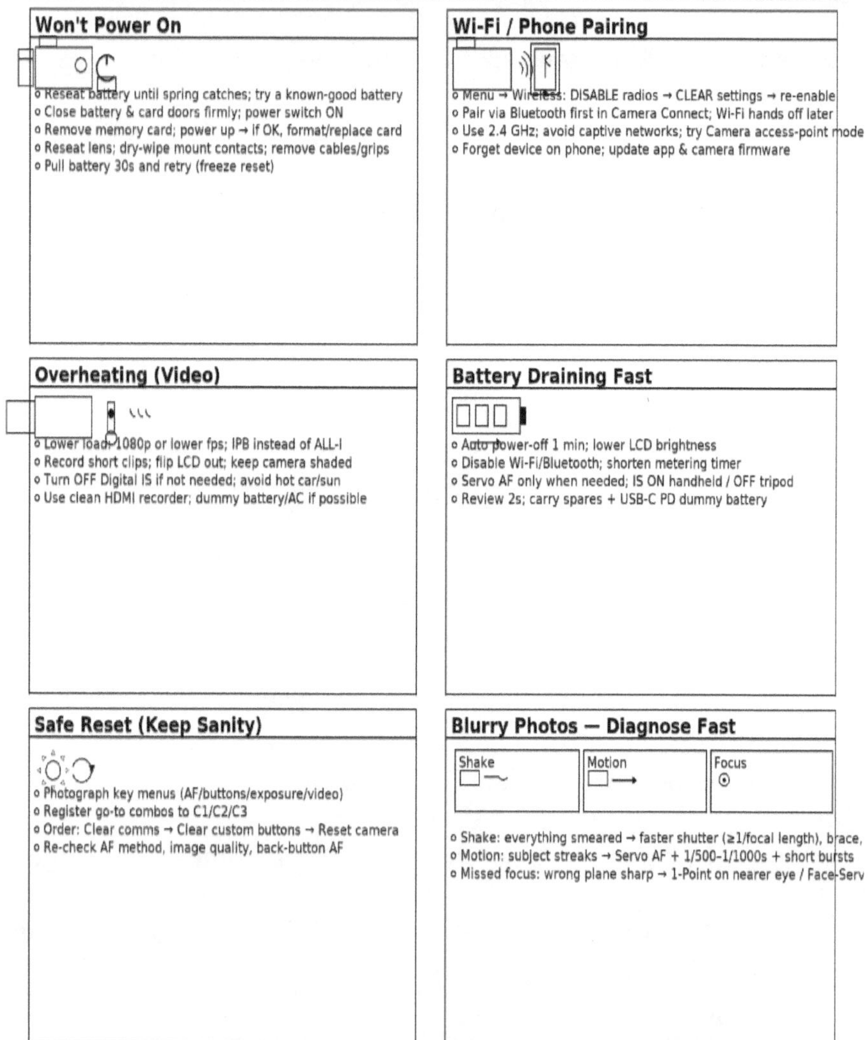

Chapter 11

Storing, Sharing & Editing Your Photos

Your photos deserve to live somewhere safer than a single SD card and look better than a straight-out-of-camera snapshot. This chapter gives you a simple, repeatable system to get images off the camera, backed up, lightly edited, and exported so they look great anywhere.

The three pathways (pick one today)

- **Fast share now (phone first):** Camera → phone via Canon Camera Connect → quick edit → share → later, archive to computer/cloud.

- **Quality first (computer):** Camera/SD card → computer → backup → cull + edit RAW → export for sharing.

- **Best of both:** Small JPEGs to phone for immediate sharing **and** full RAWs to computer/cloud the same day.

You can switch paths anytime, but consistency beats complexity. Choose the one you'll actually do after every shoot.

Getting photos off the EOS R

A) To your phone or tablet (quickest)

1. Pair once in Canon Camera Connect (Bluetooth for control, Wi-Fi for transfers).

2. On the camera: Play → choose images → Send to smartphone.

3. In the app, pick "Original size" when you want best quality; "Smaller size" for fast sharing.

Pro tips

- If you shot RAW+JPEG, send the JPEG for speed; keep the RAWs for later editing.

- In steady lighting, set WB to Daylight or Kelvin before shooting—your phone edits will be more consistent.

B) To your computer (best quality, fastest workflow)

Use one of these:

- SD card reader (fastest).

- USB-C cable from camera to computer.

- Direct Wi-Fi to a computer is possible but slower—use a cable or reader if available.

On import, create a date-based folder and rename files so you can recognize them later.

Simple, future-proof folder scheme

```
Photos/
  2025/
    2025-08-16_Lagos_Family/
      RAW/          (all .CR3 raw files)
```

```
JPEG/           (camera JPEGs, if any)

EDITS/          (exports you share)

SELECTS/        (keepers after culling)
```

File renaming pattern

```
2025-08-16_Lagos_Family_0001.CR3

2025-08-16_Lagos_Family_0002.CR3
```

Use your editor's import dialog to apply this automatically.

Never lose a photo again: the easy 3-2-1 backup

- 3 copies of your photos

- 2 different kinds of storage (e.g., internal drive + external SSD/NAS)

- 1 copy off-site (cloud)

What this looks like in real life

1. Primary: Your computer's photo drive (internal or external SSD).

2. Secondary: A second external drive or a home NAS that mirrors the Photos folder.

3. Off-site cloud: One of these always-on options:

   o A photo cloud (Google Photos, iCloud Photos, Microsoft OneDrive, Amazon Photos).

   o A file cloud (Dropbox, Backblaze, iDrive) backing up your Photos folder in full resolution.

Set and forget: Turn on automatic sync for your Photos folder so every new import is protected without extra clicks.

A quick, sane editing flow (10 minutes or less)

You don't need to become a retoucher. This is a repeatable edit recipe that works in Snapseed (free), Lightroom (mobile or desktop), Apple Photos, Google Photos, Darktable, or RawTherapee.

1. Cull first, edit second.

   o   Do one fast pass: mark keepers and obvious rejects.

   o   Aim for 10–30% keepers. The more you cull, the better your set looks.

2. Crop & straighten.

   o   Get the story tight. Level horizons. Fix tilted walls.

3. Exposure balance.

   o   Adjust Exposure until faces look natural.

   o   Tame highlights; lift shadows a touch. Avoid a muddy midtone look.

4. White balance.

   o   If skin is too cool/warm, use Temperature/Tint.

   o   In most apps, a neutral surface (gray/white) + WB picker = instant fix.

5. Presence & color.

   o   Add a little Contrast or Curve.

   o   Use Vibrance before Saturation (it protects skin tones).

- o If colors feel weird, reduce saturation instead of over-warming WB.

6. Lens corrections & sharpening.

    - o Enable Profile Corrections (vignetting/distortion).

    - o Sharpen lightly; add Noise Reduction only as needed.

7. Local tweaks (optional, huge payoff).

    - o A small brush/radial to brighten eyes or faces by +0.2–0.5 EV.

    - o A quick dehaze for hazy landscapes.

8. Save your look.

    - o Create a preset once you like the vibe. Next edits become one-click.

RAW vs JPEG

- RAW (.CR3) gives maximum flexibility (best for tricky light and big edits).

- JPEG is fine for quick share if the exposure/WB is already good.

  When in doubt, shoot RAW+JPEG: share the JPEG today, polish the RAW later.

Exporting for social without the mushy look

Most platforms re-compress images. You'll get cleaner results if you control the export.

- Color space: sRGB (always for web/social).

- Format: JPEG (8-bit), Quality ~80–90%.

- Size: A practical "always good" share size is 2048–2560 px on the long edge.

  - Portraits for feeds often look great around 1080 × 1350 px.

  - Landscape posts: 1920 × 1080 px is a safe baseline.

  - Stories/Reels: 1080 × 1920 px (vertical).

- Output sharpening: Choose "screen" / "standard" if your editor offers it—prevents the softening that happens online.

- Avoid double compression: Don't screenshot your photo; export once from your editor and upload that file.

- Metadata: If privacy matters, export without location data.

A frictionless end-to-end routine (use this after every shoot)

1. Import the same day

- Card → computer into your date-named folder.
- Optional: quick phone transfer of a few favorites for same-day sharing.

2. Back up immediately

- Confirm your cloud sync icon is active and your second drive mirrored.

3. Cull once, edit once

- Pick keepers, apply your preset, tweak exposure/WB, export.

4. Export two versions

- Share: sRGB JPEG, 2048–2560 px long edge, Q 80–90, output sharpen: screen.

- Archive: full-res JPEG or TIFF (for prints), plus the original RAW in your RAW folder.

5. Deliver or post

- Use albums (cloud or phone) with clear names—same as your folder names—so future you can find things in seconds.

Troubleshooting the workflow

- **Phone says "insufficient space":** Offload old media to cloud/drive and enable auto-upload, or send "smaller size" copies for quick sharing.

- **Computer is slow with RAWs:** Keep originals on a fast SSD. In Lightroom, build smart previews to edit smoothly on smaller machines.

- **Cloud looks different from your edit:** Re-export as sRGB JPEG (not AdobeRGB/ProPhoto).

- **Duplicates everywhere:** Let one app manage the library (e.g., Lightroom) and back that folder up; avoid importing into multiple apps.

Gear settings that help this chapter

- File numbering: Set to Continuous so file names don't reset every card.

- RAW+JPEG: Enable when you want day-one sharing with future-proof editing.

- Copyright info: Add your name/contact in-camera; it travels with every file.

Build the habit once, and your photos will always be safe, findable,

and good-looking—from card to cloud to the people who want to

see them.

CHAPTER 11 — STORING, SHARING & EDITING YOUR PHOTOS

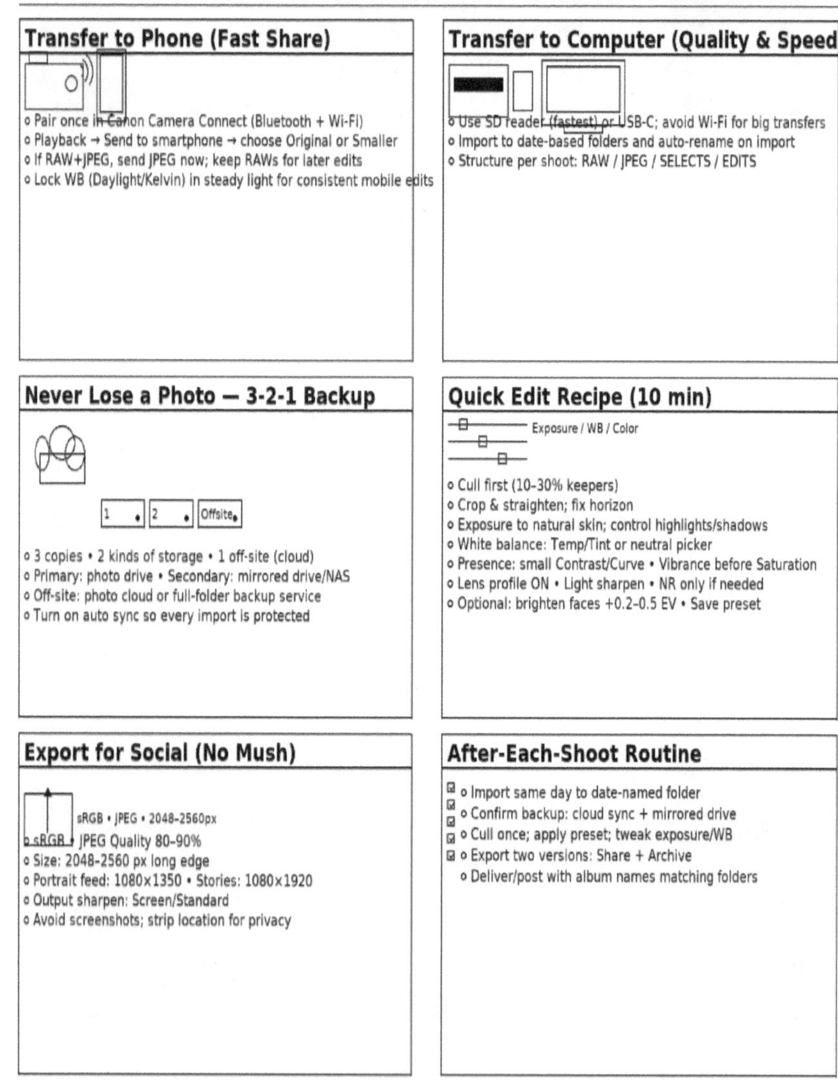

Transfer to Phone (Fast Share)

o Pair once in Canon Camera Connect (Bluetooth + Wi-Fi)
o Playback → Send to smartphone → choose Original or Smaller
o If RAW+JPEG, send JPEG now; keep RAWs for later edits
o Lock WB (Daylight/Kelvin) in steady light for consistent mobile edits

Transfer to Computer (Quality & Speed)

o Use SD reader (fastest) or USB-C; avoid Wi-Fi for big transfers
o Import to date-based folders and auto-rename on import
o Structure per shoot: RAW / JPEG / SELECTS / EDITS

Never Lose a Photo — 3-2-1 Backup

o 3 copies • 2 kinds of storage • 1 off-site (cloud)
o Primary: photo drive • Secondary: mirrored drive/NAS
o Off-site: photo cloud or full-folder backup service
o Turn on auto sync so every import is protected

Quick Edit Recipe (10 min)

Exposure / WB / Color

o Cull first (10–30% keepers)
o Crop & straighten; fix horizon
o Exposure to natural skin; control highlights/shadows
o White balance: Temp/Tint or neutral picker
o Presence: small Contrast/Curve • Vibrance before Saturation
o Lens profile ON • Light sharpen • NR only if needed
o Optional: brighten faces +0.2–0.5 EV • Save preset

Export for Social (No Mush)

sRGB • JPEG • 2048–2560px
o sRGB • JPEG Quality 80–90%
o Size: 2048–2560 px long edge
o Portrait feed: 1080×1350 • Stories: 1080×1920
o Output sharpen: Screen/Standard
o Avoid screenshots; strip location for privacy

After-Each-Shoot Routine

o Import same day to date-named folder
o Confirm backup: cloud sync + mirrored drive
o Cull once; apply preset; tweak exposure/WB
o Export two versions: Share + Archive
  o Deliver/post with album names matching folders

Chapter 12

Going Beyond the Basics

Plateaus happen. The cure isn't more gear—it's systems, projects, and a few advanced techniques you can actually repeat in the field. This chapter turns "someday" into muscle memory: custom modes you can call up blind, long-exposure recipes, focus stacking and HDR that don't feel like science class, and a video workflow you'll trust on a real shoot. Then we'll lock in a growth plan so you keep climbing.

Custom Shooting Modes: Your Three "Instant Brains"

Treat C1–C3 like presets for your future self. You'll stop diving through menus and start shooting on instinct.

How to register a custom mode (once)

1. Set the camera exactly how you want (mode, aperture/shutter, AF behavior, drive, ISO limits, button customizations, WB, etc.).

2. MENU → Custom shooting mode (C1–C3) → Register settings.

3. Choose Auto update: OFF to keep these modes locked, or ON if you want them to learn as you tweak.

Suggested setups

C1 — Portraits/People (controlled light)

- Mode: Av • Aperture: f/2–f/2.8 • Min. shutter: 1/160–1/250s (in ISO settings)
- AF: One-Shot + Face/Eye • ISO: Auto (cap 3200–6400) • WB: Kelvin/Daylight for consistent skin
- Drive: Low/Single (no machine gunning)

C2 — Action/Street (unpredictable)

- Mode: Tv • Shutter: 1/1000s (drop to 1/500s indoors)

- AF: Servo + small Zone (Face/Tracking when faces fill frame)

- ISO: Auto (cap 6400) • WB: Auto • Drive: High speed

C3 — Tripod/Landscape & Night

- Mode: M • Aperture: f/8–f/11 • ISO: 100 • Shutter: whatever the meter needs

- AF: One-Shot, 1-Point • Timer: 2-sec • IS: Off (on tripod) • WB: Kelvin for repeatable color

Now, when the moment happens, it's one click to the brain you need.

Long Exposure Without the Mystery

Silky water, empty city squares, starry skies—the secret is a stable camera, predictable math, and simple habits.

Daytime long exposure (water/clouds)

You need: tripod, remote/timer, ND filter (6-stop for subtle motion, 10-stop for dramatic), lens hood, microfiber.

Steps:

1. Compose without the ND. Focus, then switch to manual focus (so it won't hunt).

2. Meter a normal shot (say, 1/125s at f/8, ISO 100).

3. Add ND and do the math: every 1 stop doubles the exposure time.

   o Example: 10 stops from 1/125s ≈ 8 seconds (1/125 → 1/60 → 1/30 → 1/15 → 1/8 → 1/4 → 1/2 → 1s → 2s → 4s → 8s).

4. Switch to Bulb if you need >30s; use the Bulb timer (if available) or a remote.

5. IS off on tripod; 2-sec timer; shade the lens; cover the viewfinder to prevent light leaks.

6. Consider turning Long Exposure NR off to keep shooting pace (you can denoise later).

Night city light trails

- Start: f/8, ISO 100, 10–20s (adjust until trails are long but not blown).

- Focus on a mid-distance object, then MF. IS off, 2-sec timer.

- For symmetrical trails, wait for opposing traffic; press when lights enter the frame.

Stars (without tracking)

- Use the "400 rule" to avoid star trails on full frame: Shutter ≈ 400 / focal length.

  o 24 mm → ~16s; 16 mm → ~25s.

- Start: f/1.8–f/2.8, ISO 3200–6400, MF on a bright star using magnify + peaking.

- WB: 3800–4500K to keep the sky neutral, tweak later.

Focus Stacking (for razor-sharp macro & product)

Your EOS R may not have automatic focus bracketing; no problem—manual stacks are reliable.

Setup

- Tripod. Manual exposure. Manual WB (Kelvin). Manual focus.

- Use magnify + focus peaking. Consider a focusing rail for precise moves (macro).

Technique

1. Start at the nearest point that must be sharp. Take a shot.

2. Nudge focus a tiny amount deeper. Shoot.

3. Repeat until you pass the farthest critical detail (usually 10–30 frames for close macro; 3–7 for product).

4. In software (Photoshop/Helicon/Zerene): align and Auto-Blend (focus stack).

5. Keep your aperture moderate (f/5.6–f/8) to avoid diffraction—stacking provides depth.

Caution: Any movement ruins alignment. Kill fans, vibrations, and use the 2-sec timer.

HDR (High Dynamic Range) That Looks Real

Use HDR when the scene has bright skies + dark interiors and a single exposure clips either end.

Two clean paths

- **Single RAW, bright exposure:** Expose for highlights (slightly dark overall), then lift shadows in the RAW editor. Great for mild range.

- **Bracket and merge:** Use AEB (auto exposure bracketing) for **±2 EV** across 3–5 frames. Tripod if you can.

1. MENU → Exposure comp./AEB and dial ±2 EV.

2. Set Drive: High speed; hold the shutter to capture the set quickly.

3. Merge in software with Auto Align and gentle tone mapping (keep contrast natural; avoid "crunchy" halos).

Tip: If people are in the scene, shoot a bracket for background and a single exposure for people, then blend the best skin frame over the merged HDR.

Advanced Video Workflows (reliable, repeatable)

Think in deliverables first (YouTube? client? family film?)—then lock the chain end-to-end.

1) Project setup

- Resolution/FPS:

- o Talking-head/films: 4K 24/25p (cinematic cadence).

  - o Tutorials/travel: 4K 30p.

  - o Slow motion: 1080p 60p (interpret to 24/30p later).

- Shutter rule: ~1/(2 × fps) (24p→1/50, 30p→1/60, 60p→1/125).

- WB: Fix it (Kelvin/Daylight). Avoid Auto WB shifts.

2) Picture style & exposure

- If your EOS R has Canon Log, enable it for more grading latitude; expose to protect highlights and add a C-Log LUT in post.

- No Log? Use Neutral or Faithful, turn contrast/sharpening down a notch for a flatter, gradable file.

- Use histogram and highlight warnings. If your body supports zebras, set ~95–100% for clipping.

3) Autofocus that doesn't hunt

- **AF method:** Face/Tracking for people; otherwise a small area.

- **AF speed/tracking sensitivity:** Slow it slightly so the camera transitions gently instead of racking.

- **Plan A:** Pre-focus where action happens. **Plan B:** If AF wobbles, switch to manual with peaking and magnify.

4) Motion & stability

- Lens IS helps. Digital IS adds crop/processing—use it sparingly.

- For handheld: tuck elbows, breathe, move like you're on rails; shoot short, steady takes.

- Walking shots: hold at 35 mm, bend knees, move heel-to-toe. Or use a small monopod as a "poor man's gimbal."

5) Audio that feels pro

- Plug a shotgun on-camera for ambient clarity; use a lavalier for talking heads.

- Set peaks around −12 dB. Monitor with headphones. Kill wind filter indoors.

6) Managing heat and files

- Prefer IPB for smaller files/less heat; ALL-I is heavier.

- Record short clips, flip the LCD out from the body, and shade the camera.

- For longer shoots, consider HDMI out to an external recorder and/or a dummy battery for cooler, continuous power.

7) Post workflow that won't choke your laptop

- Create proxies (1080p) from 4K for smooth editing.

- In Log, apply a technical LUT, then tweak exposure/contrast/saturation—small moves.

- Export: H.264/H.265, sRGB, bitrate matched to platform (YouTube handles high bitrates; social prefers smaller).

Keep Improving: A System You'll Actually Use

Weekly "10-Frame Projects"

- Pick a narrow brief: "Hands & light", "Reflections at dusk", "Candid portraits at 35 mm".

- Limit yourself to one lens and ten frames. Constraints force growth.

Reverse-Engineer Photos You Love

- Ask: Where is the light? How big? What's the key angle?

- Recreate it in your space with a window, a sheet as a diffuser, a reflector—whatever you have.

Build a Feedback Loop

- Print one photo a week at 8×10". Paper reveals flaws screens hide.

- Seek critique (local club, online groups, a trusted friend who shoots). Listen for patterns.

Make a Shot Log (3 bullets per shoot)

- What worked, what failed, what I'll try next time.

- Revisit before your next session—now you're learning on purpose.

Keep your curiosity paid up

- Watch a tutorial, then immediately replicate one scene.

- Assist a local photographer for a day; you'll absorb more in hours than weeks of scrolling.

- Schedule "play days" monthly: no pressure, just experiments (gels, prisms, shadows on walls, long-exposure nights).

A 5-Minute "Beyond Basics" Ritual (before any serious shoot)

1. Pick your mode: C1 (people), C2 (motion), or C3 (tripod).
2. Check exposure triangle for the goal (freeze, depth, or time).
3. Fix WB if the light is steady.
4. Choose AF area for the subject (small & precise vs. Face/Tracking).
5. Make three quick tests: wide establishing, medium, tight detail—then commit.

Mastery is less about secret settings and more about repeatable choices. Set your modes, run the recipes, keep the weekly projects alive—and you won't just leave beginner level; you'll stay out of it.

Custom Shooting Modes (C1/C2/C3)

o Register once: MENU → Custom shooting mode → Register
o C1 People: Av • f/2–2.8 • Min 1/160–1/250 • Face/Eye
o C2 Action: Tv • 1/1000s (1/500 indoor) • Servo + small Zone
o C3 Tripod: M • f/8–f/11 • ISO 100 • 2s timer • IS Off
o Auto update OFF = locked; ON = learns your tweaks

Long Exposure (Day & Night)

o Day: ND 6–10 stops • Focus first then MF • IS Off on tripod
o Math: each stop doubles time (1/125 → 10-stop ≈ 8s)
o City trails: f/8 • ISO 100 • 10–20s
o Stars (no tracker): 400 ÷ focal length → shutter (24mm ≈ 16s)
o Cover viewfinder; 2s timer; shade lens

Focus Stacking (Macro/Product)

o Tripod • Manual exposure/WB/focus • Magnify + peaking
o Shoot nearest sharp → nudge deeper → repeat
o Typical: 10–30 frames macro • 3–7 product
o Keep f/5.6–f/8; stack/align/merge in software

HDR That Looks Real

o Single RAW: expose for highlights; lift shadows later
o Bracket: AEB ±2 EV (3–5 frames); Drive: High speed
o Tripod preferred; Auto Align; gentle tone mapping
o People? Merge background + paste best skin frame

Advanced Video Workflow

24/30/60p
1/(2×fps)

o Deliverable first: 4K 24/25p film • 4K 30p tutorial • 1080 60p slow-mo
o Shutter ≈ 1/(2×fps) • Fix WB (Kelvin) • Zebra 95–100%
o C-Log + LUT if available; else Neutral/Faithful lowered contrast/sharpen
o AF: slower AF speed; small area; pre-focus • Short steady takes
o Post: proxies for smooth edit; small grades; export H.264/265 sRGB

Keep Learning (No Plateau)

o Weekly 10-frame projects with one lens + tight brief
o Reverse-engineer favorites: light direction/size/angle
o Print 8×10 weekly; seek critique; track recurring notes
o Shot log after each session: worked / failed / next
o Monthly play days: gels, prisms, long-exposure nights

Bonus

Quick Settings Cheat Sheets

Why this matters: When you're in the field, you don't have time to dig through menus or second-guess exposure. These one-page recipes give you exact starting points you can call up in seconds—and a shortcut path to any menu item you'll ever need on the EOS R. No tables, no fluff, just real settings and moves.

Cheat Sheet 1 — Portraits (Individuals, Couples, Small Groups)

Goal: natural skin tones, sharp eyes, clean backgrounds.

Default setup (store as C1 if you like):

- Mode: Av

- Aperture: f/2–f/2.8 (single subject), f/4–f/5.6 (groups)

- Minimum shutter (ISO settings): 1/160–1/250 s

- ISO: Auto (cap 3200–6400)

- AF: One-Shot + Face/Eye Detection ON (switch to Servo for kids/pets)

- WB: Daylight or Kelvin in steady light; Auto WB if light changes

- Drive: Single or Low-speed; avoid spray-and-pray indoors

Fast dial moves in the moment:

- Background too busy? Open aperture one stop and step closer.

- Subject moving? Servo AF + raise minimum shutter to 1/500 s.

- Mixed light? Kill indoor bulbs or switch to Auto WB and fix later.

Light & color tips:

- Turn faces 45° toward the window/sky; lift shadows with a white card.

- Keep skin natural: prefer Vibrance over heavy Saturation later.

Quick fixes:

- Eyes soft → use 1-Point AF on the nearer eye, recompose gently.
- Orange cast indoors → set Kelvin ~3200–3800K or take a custom WB.

Shot list to cover yourself: hero waist-up → tight headshot → full length → candid laughter → hands & details.

Cheat Sheet 2 — Landscapes (Day, Golden Hour, Travel Vistas)

Goal: maximum detail, controlled highlights, clean composition.

Default setup (great for C3):

- Mode: M

- Aperture: f/8–f/11

- ISO: 100

- Shutter: whatever the meter requires (use histogram, protect highlights)

- AF: One-Shot, 1-Point; or MF with magnify for critical foreground

- Stability: Tripod, 2-sec timer, IS OFF on lens when on tripod

- WB: Daylight or Kelvin for consistent color across a series

Helpful extras:

- Circular polarizer to deepen sky and cut glare on water/leaves.

- ND filter for silky water or moving clouds.

Fast dial moves:

- Bright sky, dark land? Expose for the sky and lift land later, or shoot a ±2 EV bracket to merge.

- Need more foreground depth? Focus a third into the scene, not infinity.

Quick fixes:

- Wind blur in grass/trees → raise shutter and ISO; catch calmer moments between gusts.

- Flat color at midday → look for backlight edges or wait for golden hour.

Shot list: wide establishing → mid-range with strong foreground → vertical version → detail textures → panoramic sweep.

Cheat Sheet 3 — Low-Light & Night (Indoors, City at Night, Stars)

Goal: sharp subjects with manageable noise, controlled motion blur.

Handheld recipe (people indoors, events):

- Mode: Fv or Tv

- Shutter: 1/125–1/250 s (kids 1/500 s)

- Aperture: as wide as your lens allows (f/1.8–f/2.8)

- ISO: Auto (don't fear 6400 if it saves the shot)

- AF: Servo + Face/Eye for people

- WB: Auto, or Kelvin if the light is steady

Tripod recipe (night scenes, light trails):

- Mode: M

- Aperture: f/5.6–f/8 (city), f/8–f/11 (light trails)

- ISO: 100–200

- Shutter: 10–20 s for trails; longer if you want denser lines

- Stability: Tripod, IS OFF, 2-sec timer, cover viewfinder to prevent light leaks

Stars (no star tracker):

- Shutter $\approx$ 400 ÷ focal length (full frame) $\rightarrow$ 24 mm $\approx$ 16 s

- Aperture: f/1.8–f/2.8

- ISO: 3200–6400

- Focus: manual on a bright star with magnify; WB 3800–4500K

Quick fixes:

- Grainy? Expose a touch brighter (without clipping) and reduce noise later.

- Color casts from streetlights? Set Kelvin or correct in RAW.

Cheat Sheet 4 — Video (Talking Head, Travel B-roll, Slow-Mo)

Goal: stable, well-exposed footage with reliable focus and clean audio.

Core settings:

- Resolution / FPS:
  - Talking head / cinematic: 4K 24/25p
  - Tutorials / travel: 4K 30p

- Slow-motion: 1080p 60p (interpret to 24/30 in editing)

- Shutter rule: ~1/(2 × fps) → 24p ≈ 1/50, 30p ≈ 1/60, 60p ≈ 1/125

- Picture: C-Log if available (grade with a LUT). No Log? Use Neutral/Faithful, nudge contrast/sharpening down.

- WB: Fix it (Kelvin/Daylight). Avoid Auto WB shifts mid-clip.

- AF that behaves: Face/Tracking for people; otherwise small AF area; slow AF speed and "locked-on" tracking to prevent hunting.

- Stability: short, steady takes; elbows tucked; Digital IS sparingly (it adds crop/processing).

- Audio: shotgun mic for ambient clarity or lav for voice; set peaks around −12 dB; monitor with headphones.

Quick fixes:

- Flicker under LEDs → try 1/50 or 1/100 (50 Hz regions) or 1/60 or 1/120 (60 Hz).

- Overheating risk → shorter clips, flip LCD out from the body, prefer IPB over ALL-I, consider HDMI to external recorder.

"Memory in Your Fingers" — EOS R Shortcut Navigation (No tables, just paths that stick)

Build a My Menu page so the settings you actually change live under the green star. Then learn the three fastest ways to move: the Q button, the MODE + Main Dial, and M-Fn cycles.

First, create your "My Menu"

- MENU → My Menu (green star) → Add items.

- Add the ones you'll use weekly (you can reorder later):

Core shooting items:

- Image quality (RAW / RAW+JPEG)

- ISO speed settings → set Minimum shutter speed

- Exposure comp./AEB (for HDR brackets)

- White balance (including Kelvin)

- Picture Style (or C-Log if available)

- AF operation (One-Shot / Servo)

- AF method (1-Point / Zone / Face Detect)

- Subject to detect → People; Eye detection ON

- Drive mode (single, low, high speed)

- Anti-flicker shoot.

- Silent shutter (only if you know the rolling-shutter trade-offs)

Video essentials:

- Movie recording size / frame rate

- High frame rate (if your body offers it)

- Movie digital IS

- Sound recording (manual level)

- Headphone volume (if supported)

Tripod / long-exposure helpers:

- Bulb timer (if available)

- Long exposure NR (toggle as needed)

- Interval timer (timelapse)

Customization & maintenance:

- Customize buttons (set AF-ON for back-button AF, assign Control Ring)

- Customize dials (put ISO somewhere you love)

- Touch & drag AF (if you use the EVF)

- Wi-Fi/Bluetooth settings (pair/clear)

- Save/load settings on card

- Reset camera (last resort)

- Firmware (check for updates)

Muscle-memory moves you'll actually use

- **Q** → the quick control grid: change AF method, WB, Picture Style, drive, metering, and more without diving into tabs.

- **MODE + Main Dial** → swap M/Av/Tv/Fv instantly; then the same dial adjusts the key variable for that mode.

- **M-Fn** (top button) → cycles through ISO → Drive → AF → WB → Exposure Comp; spin the front dial to change, rear dial to choose a different category.

- **AF-ON** held = continuous focus even in One-Shot (back-button AF habit).

- **INFO** cycles display overlays; magnify to nail manual focus on static scenes.

- **Set your C1/C2/C3** once and stop menu fishing in changing light.

How to print and carry these

- Keep these four recipes as literal one-pagers: Portraits, Landscapes, Low-Light, Video.

- Print in grayscale on A5 or 6×9"; laminate or slip into your bag.

- Or export as simple PNGs for your phone so they're in your camera roll when you need them.

Quick "oh-no" resets (just in case)

- Everything feels wrong? Switch to your **C1/C2/C3** baseline for the scenario.

- AF hunting? Face/Eye OFF → 1-Point, focus on the eye/edge, recompose gently.

- Motion blur creeping in? Raise minimum shutter or switch to Tv 1/500 s and let ISO climb.

- Color weird? Kelvin (steady light) or Auto WB (changing light), fix the rest in RAW.

Acknowledgments

Creating this guide has been a journey made possible by more than just technical know-how—it's been powered by community, curiosity, and countless moments behind the lens.

First, to the everyday photographers—beginners, seniors, travelers, vloggers, and creators—who inspired this book: thank you. Your questions, frustrations, and breakthroughs shaped every chapter and reminded me why clarity matters.

To the online communities, forum contributors, and real-world Canon EOS R users who openly shared their challenges and insights: your stories breathed realism into this work.

A special thanks to my editorial team, design collaborators, and research assistants for helping bring structure, precision, and visual support to every page.

Finally, to the readers picking up this book—whether you're just unboxing your Canon R or finally ready to leave auto mode behind—thank you for trusting this guide as part of your journey. May it help you create images that not only look beautiful, but feel meaningful.

Keep shooting. Keep learning. The world is waiting through your lens.

About The Author

Randy Osborn is a trusted name in the world of camera education, known for transforming complex gear manuals into simple, step-by-step guides that anyone can understand. With over a decade of experience working hands-on with leading camera systems—from Sony and Canon to Nikon, Leica, and more—Randy has helped thousands of photographers, content creators, and everyday users get the most out of their cameras without the overwhelm.

Driven by a passion for accessible learning, Randy creates user-friendly books that strip away the jargon and focus on real-world usage. Whether you're shooting your first vlog, learning manual mode for the first time, or simply trying to take better family photos, Randy's guides are designed to make every setting click.

Each book combines clear instruction, practical tips, and

relatable language, making it easy for beginners and seasoned hobbyists alike to master their gear and capture life with confidence.

When he's not writing, Randy enjoys field testing new camera releases, hosting beginner-friendly workshops, and exploring hidden photography gems across the globe.

Join the journey to sharper skills and smarter shooting—one page at a time.